WORDS FROM A POET'S SOUL

FIRST EDITION

Marjorie E. Edwards

Cover design: Michael Tayler, Upstairs Design Group
Interior design: Marjorie E. Edwards
Author's photo: Roy Sweetland Photography
Editor: Foyah Z. Freeman, Jr.

Library of Congress Control Number: TXU 1-752-060
ISBN-978-0615681191

Email: jemarge58@yahoo.com
Web: www.marjorieeedwards.com
Web:https://www.facebook.com/marjorie.edward3

Marjorie E. Edwards
Words From A Poet's Soul

Printed in the United States of America

FROM THE AUTHOR

I am truly blessed to dedicate this book to all as an inspirational, influential, and motivational gift that comes naturally from my heart. A collection of inspirational poems that cover the spectrum of life, from a Jamaican perspective. It is filled with creative ideas to encourage, motivate, soothe and inspire humor to refresh the mind with relaxation while providing therapeutic energy. Fun and laughter captures each moment.

The way I receive it, I deliver it. A passion, I hope, that will be shared and enjoyed by all who turn the pages of this book. In addition, I pray to God that each passage will be a blessing to the hearts of those who read them.

Marjorie E. Edwards
2012

TABLE OF CONTENTS

A MOTHER'S LOVE SECURES

A

Mother's love to all is free,
Out of her heart she gives
To others to shelter them to be,
Her very own today, tomorrow, and forever.
Ever more nurturing, strengthening, and desiring,
Redeeming, inspiring, representing, and ready to fulfill;
Solacing in wisdom and harmony with prayers.

Longed in her bosom,
Only love created without ransom.
Very dear and priceless to be known,
Extending in time and space, not to be outgrown.

Shows with her kindness, rich in mercies, and forgiveness,
Evolves around the desolate in comfort and togetherness.
Communicates with patience, peace, and rewards in
Unity, that portrays in her emblem of all reasoning.
Reaching out to all, matters not whom being her own offspring!
Everlasting attributes, unconditionally she gives in all her care,
She supplies in purity, this precious affection with all her heart.

Author: Marjorie E. Edwards
Created: March 1, 2011

Dedicated to all the Mothers

3

DEAREST FRIEND

Dearest friend,
One will never understand,
How much to us, it means,
To see each other's happy smiling faces again!

To realize we were, since
From the earlier days, we expected to last.
Had it only been left to me that night,
I would have surely passed without a sight.

When I was asked to say a prayer,
I gathered lovingly, everyone in a humble manner.
We prayed God to bless the home and household man,
And begged Him to place us all into His heavenly plan.

When I heard someone called my name,
Knew it had to be one from my childhood game.
Surprised, we hugged, rocked, then faithfully shared,
"Oh dear, what are you doing here?"

Boy! How much we have changed over the years.
Now this encourages passion of happy tears!
Just to hear my name with such enhanced beam;
To me, it was more like a dramatic dream!

Over the years, I thought where to find
All my friends from the olden times,
Think about all our rising dawns,
And prayed God to help our pleading psalms.

Reminiscing the days we played together,
Walked to school in the hot, cold, and stormy weather,
All thoughts, poems, and skills, we learned it all,
Even with the book, "Moon on a Rainbow Shawl."

Good decisions made in life often worked well,
Had I not taken the time off from my busy spell,
To join in this celebration of ringing birthday bells,
Then I wouldn't be fulfilled with such intriguing thrills.

An achievement to be grateful for
Seeing each other again, come this far!
Thanking God for His blessings and merciful days,
Forever, we are now with families to stay!

Author: Marjorie E. Edwards
Created: April 15, 2011

Dedicated to my childhood friends

"Happy Birthday Bliss!"

MY FIRST BABY BOY

Today, I'm blessed with another bundle of joy,
As I reached out to take my first baby boy,
We bonded for the last two-hundred and eighty days,
And I'm certainly sure you've inherited most of my ways.

You came on this Christmas morn,
Where there were only lanterns to keep us warm.
Angels presence bring peace and comforting charm,
God's gifted possession, with Him there is no harm.

Healthy little feet with strength like a lion born,
Reminds me, that here lies your first playpen dorm,
Someday, you will grow up to be a big strong man!
And you will be grown from mom's cuddling hands.

Your sensitive eyes that caught my soundless peek,
To prolong your sleep, I ran for a retreat;
Then the sounds of your hands, voice, and feet,
Commanding mom, it's now time to eat.

With your presence, life was nonetheless of a big task,
Especially, when I made your first long pants to dance!
I vowed one day, that another you would never wear,
After you went and kicked the fifth one torn.

Our breads were always at a loss,
When you teamed up with your pet and best friend,
Together, you would pull the tablecloth to toss,
Then would sit and mumble until it's loss.

My son to me will always belong,
And this poem will be my special song.
With embracing time of life's challenging soar;
You hold a special place at my heart's door.

Mom's heart sings in sweet memories,
For the gift of love, a son to me was born.
God's precious love beyond all boundaries,
On that Merry, Merry Christmas morn!

Author: Marjorie E. Edwards
Created: December 25, 2009

Dedicated to my first son Gerald

A
gift for
Christmas

7

MY FAMILY

I like to talk most times,
As a mother, with those children of mine.
Now that everybody has their own life,
Can hardly find time for my worrying strife.

My children, I love them all dearly,
And wish that, for me time can spear.
Constantly calling upon my daughter
To lodge complaints on the others.

The thing is, I cannot talk
About one or two and leave out the others.
She listens attentively, here and there,
Then says "Mi no business wid yuh an yuh Pinckney dem dear!"

I wondered what she really meant by that
Does she not remember that she is one?
Or not to talk with her about the others,
Or is it that she just can't be bothered?

I have sweet children.
But not all the time we are the best of friends.
They are all at a different age,
And each learns at a different stage.

My life, I share evenly with them,
Each one to me, special time to spend,
All share with me, no matter what weather,
It is a joy, for mommy to have her children together.

Author: Marjorie E. Edwards
Created: November 5, 2011

MY FRIENDS, EACH A TREASURE

My friends, each a real treasure.
Devotional duties we share to inspire,
And sincere qualities without fear,
They are like breaths of fresh air!

It is said, that one may travel and find new friends,
Friends who will associate with struggles and strife,
But the best friends you will ever have,
Are those who journey along with your life!

My friends will always be the future.
Never will become the past,
It is like a bonding team all secure,
Because true friendships will last.

Positive revival we will ever seek!
The negative word we will never hear,
By applying drips of charmed thoughts,
To outdo the negative sword.

Men, women, boy, and girlfriends,
Old friends, new friends, and willing friends,
Who are, and soon will become nurturing strength.
Even, in this place, there is quite an intrigue to share.

Moreover, when the day shall have ended,
And the tenor of humorous courses complete,
Remember, because of our humble presence,
Life is so much worth the living.

That our friendship has scored the measure:
In addition, the fulfilled satisfaction is guaranteed.
By validating the joy as our everlasting treasure,
To you all, I write this poem with the greatest pleasure.

Author: Marjorie E. Edwards
Created: June 3, 2008

Dedicated to my friends

Friendships
Always
And
Forever

MY OWN BABY GIRL

A beautiful blessing and a whole new world,
Was that day, when I held my own baby girl!
Beautiful creation of God's most perfect love,
That special peace that comes from above.

Her grateful shining eyes greeting mine,
And darling little feet both so fine.
With clenched fists, almost ready for a fight,
And hungry lips to receive the target site.

Her body movement dances to a new sublime,
To find that special warmth she had just left behind,
Just the touch of these soft little hands,
Will someday teach mom how to be strong!

My friend, my joy with all the pride I share,
A job well done with humbleness and submissive care,
My nine-months' journey with all the love abounding,
I'm blessed the day you came to share my surroundings.

A gift of grace that solemnly embraces me!
You came for a reason in all due season,
I am glad that the heavenly love unfurled,
For you to be a part of my life's world.

My own baby girl!
My own baby girl!
I bless the day you came,
To share my world.

Author: Marjorie E. Edwards
Created: April 20, 2010
Dedicated to my daughter, Tashalee

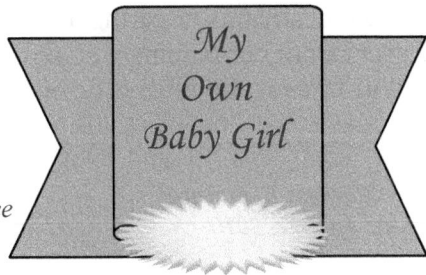

My Own Baby Girl

PARENTS

Do you ever wonder how parents ought to be special?
Moreover, for us, they are always meeting our essentials,
To exercise the memoir of each character defining naturally,
In addition to all the tasks, they are far more than just usual.

Most of our parents virtually had nothing,
However, we all came out to be something.
I knew quite a few who were poor,
Yet, they made it possible for us to enter and exit a door.

With much dedication, to work hard to provide,
And at no time ever left us on the outside.
They showed pleasure to achieve and were never reluctant,
Because for them, we were all very important.

With unconditional love, they were always willing
To take up the burden of numerous giving,
First to second, down to great-grand kings and queens,
As long as it fulfills ambitious family dreams.

Value of togetherness, gracefully we will say, 'Mom,'
For the power and authority, proudly we will color him, 'Dad,'
Or in different scenarios wherever it may apply,
It was still a tough job to maintain all the supplies.

From all unceasing reservoirs of 'Charismatic virtues,'
That flow in streams of caring and superior values.
Entrusted from our parents who will always be special,
And will forever and always be our very own essentials.

Author: Marjorie E. Edwards
Created: April 22, 2010

PRECIOUS LITTLE ONE OF OURS

Precious little one of ours,
Adding one more jewel to shine,
From "You Lord," comes always the best,
Today his presence provides soothing rest

All eyes scanned his gentle body structure,
Praising God for his perfect creative features,
With waving hands, hollering cries, and kicking feet,
No doubt, he is going to look a lot like mom.

As I placed him close by my side,
I vowed, this is where he will always abide,
Someday when the time is right for him to decide,
He will gain the distance from mom's cuddling hide.

Another baby gained!
As I looked out at the falling rain,
And if I had to do it again,
I would never, ever fear the pain.

Now, been a proud mother of all three,
More work and play, I'll never be able to go free.
After the families came to share their views,
I will be left all alone with my baby blues.

Now it is time for his bubbles and beauty care,
Sis, with her help we can depend on for sure,
After his dining chores when he had had enough,
In his cot, he would be placed and covered all up.

Such an adorable sight to see,
For me so proud, again a mommy to be!
So let us go and get some rest,
While baby sleeps to his humblest zest.

Your best playmate was older Brother 'J,'
When he challenged you to the test,
Upon my hips you would hop up and stay,
Then laugh at him to your uttermost best.

When it comes time to prove your point,
With anyone, you did not have to fight,
Mom being your first and only confidant,
Will surely listen and verdict your rights.

Sharing mommy's job was a great start,
Especially, when it begins at 1:30 a.m. sharp,
If it meant for you to play your only part,
By claiming the first baked beef patty tart.

With older, Brother 'J,' you played karate for fun,
Until this day, my son, you are still our number one!
In victory, you claimed your well-earned crown,
By shouting, "See what little boy to big boy done!"

For you, going to school was a great delight,
Especially when you took over the football field,
And with a score of a whopping 4.0 spill,
After you've done your creative writing skill.

Someday when all grown up from my side,
On my hips, you will not need to take your ride,
Nor these hands, to secure your tiny strides,
Or my presence to play your seek and hide.

But, in mom's heart those special days will always remain,
And the proud memories will reminisce over and over again;
It's just like feeling your strengthened, poised feet,
Dancing to the rhythms of our very own hearts beat.

Author: Marjorie E. Edwards
Created: December, 2009

Dedicated to my second son Larenio

SINCE HE WENT AWAY

When he decided to go,
All the memories followed him.
He did not say, "Baby let's try,
Together we'll work it anyway."

They had a family to share,
And they vowed that they'd take care,
Could not afford to live without,
So she took the night shift work.

Since he left and went away,
No more tears, had she displayed.
She had more time to plan her way,
And she'd been busy until today.

With God's grace, she handled it,
She couldn't run from her problems, man!
But does he know how old his children are?
The youngest now turns twenty-three.

So now that life has changed,
Here's time for him to rearrange,
He didn't choose his sanity then,
Why the heck, now come to pretend?

Now he is back to see them again,
Too late now for his surprise spend,
Had endorsed the fact that he was gone,
The day he left and went away.

So, fathers please stay around,
Provide your children with a home,
They will choose to love just the same,
Doesn't have to be only to those who carry your name.

Mothers, please keep your ground,
Make your children all a home,
They will choose to love just the same,
Doesn't have to be only to those who came from your womb.

Author: Marjorie E. Edwards
Created: February 2, 2011

THE REALITIES OF THE CAT

Hi, I'm Teddy, Harry, Percy, and Freddy, a real fame!
They called me the cat with multiple names.
I'm Mr. Cool who knows it all, but sometimes what?
I don't sit around or play with toys all day in fact.

I do not in the least favor heights,
If the ground is too far away from my sight,
I stay away from that dreadful fright,
Even great climbers often succumb to sudden plight.

Most times, I do not like to be bothered.
Especially in the cold weather,
Do not touch my ears or my head,
When I'm, curl up, in my mistresses' bed!

I like being patted on the back,
And get all the goodies from his backpack;
Whenever she combs away all my loosened hair,
That's too much loving; it gets me a little scary.

I took my chance and bolted through the door,
Less trouble I thought, it will be on the first floor,
Where the grounds are all laid and the trees ascend,
There, I will practice my climbing skills.

I know for me, they do worry,
But to get back I'm in no hurry!
They feed me all too very well,
And my safety is sure, I can tell.

Among the thorns, I will get my rest.
Where I'm at, they will not be aware,
And often times, on them, I will take a peek.
I will stay right here and watch everyone stare!

18

But now I'm getting hungry, worn, and torn,
Looking at all these insects running around,
I'm trembling, I'm wet, and I'm terribly cold,
Being Mr. Cool cat, I'm not so bold.

From a reliable source,
I knew the time he would leave the house,
So with my cold tail up in the air,
Up the stairs, I'll stroll past the neighbor's chair.

And with a flip from my tail
To him I must prevail.
Go on, go ahead to work my dear,
When you get back, I shall be right here!

Now I live in a big house on the first floor,
Lots of space with front and back doors,
The pool I love the most,
And every morning I even order my toast.

For me, there are lots of spaces to reign,
I must choose others to entertain,
I hope it will not be much of a hazard,
To bring home a couple of live lizards.

My duty is to patrol throughout the night,
Never again, I will never be afraid of heights,
In this huge backyard, I will always stay in sight,
Finally, finally, and finally, they all got it right!

Author: Marjorie E. Edwards
Created: January 31, 201

The Family Cat.
Teddy, Harry and Percy
The cat with multiple names

YOU ARE MY REASON

You are my reason
To come this way again,
I just couldn't give up it seems,
From all the memories and poetic dreams,
So you are my reason to come this way again.

In natural and intriguing ways,
A gift sure to last for entire days,
Abundantly stored is as much to stay,
Life's interest speaks in charismatic sway,
Hence, you are my reason to come this way again.

In any season endows,
The best in you for me to grow,
With the vision of reflection in expressions so deep,
Life's journey made you mine, always to keep,
So you are my reason to come this way again.

For a special friend,
I will devote the time again and again,
Heading for a destination so giftedly gain,
The fulfilling reassurance allot to ascertain,
Indeed, you are my reason to come this way again.

And oh, I must include our mobile reliant friend,
Who waits patiently to allocate with the best she knows,
She shines, glows, and glitters as she turns her key to go,
In illustrious comfort, she rolls in safety of soothing melody.
She knows you are our very reason to come this way again.

Author: Marjorie E. Edwards
Created: July 13 - July 14, 2011

YOU SAW THE CHANCE FOR ME

So impressed with the messages I unfold,
Knew it was coming from deep within my soul,
And gave me a chance to air my way,
So you saw the chance for me to get this far.

With good intentions, you gave me a number,
Didn't think it was too much of any bother,
Didn't even know me that much by far,
But you saw that gift in me, to become a star.

I know you must have done it for many others,
So please take my hand my dear brother,
Said it often times of how proud you are,
You saw the chance for me to become, a star.

So now I'm right here where I stand,
Hoping you will come now to take my hand,
And I know that I'm grateful to you by far,
Because you gave the chance for me to become a star.

The many times you encouraged the effort,
All at the same time with complimenting support,
You reached out and showed me the way!
Yes, you saw that gift in me to become a star.

Author: Marjorie E. Edwards
Created: February 1, 2011

Thanksgiving

AS I ARRIVED IN THIS NEW TOWN

As I arrived in this new town,
To start a life all on my own,
Twenty-five dollars in my old purse,
I pray my God, His love disburse.

No mama, no papa around,
No special gifts to call my own!
Just a grandma who took care of her own,
Thank God, today I'm fully grown!

I worked so hard to build my grade,
To venture all in special aid,
With grandma now on the other side,
Cautiously I'll take my stride.

Didn't know how I was going to withstand,
All I know, grandma's memory lives on,
In my heart, to help me carry on,
And my God will take the rest into His hand.

Oh! What a blessing for new found friends,
Those who are sincere will never pretend,
Today I'm blessed, so blessed, so blessed,
I'm here to sing and share my song.

Author: Marjorie E. Edwards
Created: June 14, 2011

DEAR LORD GIFT ME

I am so grateful,
For the gift of life to go on,
Because on the cross a sacrifice,
With His life, He gave for all.

Lord, with your life on Calvary,
O gift me, unto Thee I pray!
Help me to use my talent sway,
Unto Your Glory, where I will stay.

So many blessings we take for granted,
For us Lord, Thou always providing,
Help us with our assurance be,
Let us to Thy Glory see.

We come to know You Dear Lord
The initiator of Thy Holy word,
Help that we will submit to the cause,
And from Thee will never take a pause.

What wonders of Your love can we do without?
Realms of blessed mercies Thou grant us throughout,
We beseech Thee, Dear Lord, of the things we need,
From Your supply, in gratitude we praise Thee to succeed!

Lord with Your life on Calvary,
O gift us, unto Thee we pray!
Help us to use our talent sway,
Unto Your Glory, where we will stay.

Author: Marjorie E. Edwards
Created: March 19, 2011

DEAR LORD THANK YOU

I am so grateful,
For my presence in life today,
The many, many blessings
Through His love He gives to stay.

Oh Dear Lord, thank You,
For all the things You do,
Thank You for pardoning me through,
Thank You for my life renewed!

I find myself leaning
Towards Your merciful care,
I need the strength in beseeching,
When I pray Your name in Psalms!

My heart in humble submission,
Rendering to Thee with permission,
Such a soothing and comforting calm,
When I call Your name in Psalms!

All praises to Thee in thanksgiving,
With glory and honor to Thee!
I pray Dear Lord not to leave me,
Let me sing Your name in Psalms!

Author: Marjorie E. Edwards
Created: May 21, 2011

HOW LONG

Shattered by life's heavy burden worries,
My eyes suppressed with tears for comfort,
My body succumbed to the turbulent fear,
My mind is filled with evading forces.

My God, how long, how far there is to go?
How much of this journey, shall I come to know?
The nights I spent all echoing my woes,
My Lord, I know now that only Thou will secure.

I must erase the past that evil has done me,
And count my blessings now for sure,
You give unconditionally for it to be,
Much easier for me to endure.

Oh! Loyalty of love through endless boundaries,
For us, You allowed enough to reproof,
The power of choice that helps us to rebound,
Your grace and Your mercies will see us through.

Author: Marjorie E. Edwards
Created: May 1, 2009

I CRY BECAUSE I KNOW WHY

I cry because I know why,
With my emotions run high,
I cry because I only know why,
When life's trials dawn on me.

I pray because I know why,
Seeking God's mercy from on high,
I pray because I only know why,
When life's trials dawn on me.

I won't question my God with why,
Because He'll fix it even before I try,
And his comfort he will not deny,
When life's trials dawn on me.

I smile because I know why,
My prayers to 'Him' not been in vain.
I smile because I only know why,
When life's trials dawn on me.

I share because I know why,
Faith has taught me always to try,
I share because I only know why,
When life's trials dawn on me.

I sing because I know my song,
God's love for me, that makes me so strong,
I sing because I only know why,
When life's trials, dawn on me.

Author: Marjorie E. Edwards
Created: April 18, 2011

PRAYERS TO ATTEND YOU

Years of decent morals been taught,
To mold and fashion a heart be brought,
Expectations that will be utilized,
When the demons arrive to socialize.

In place of nothing else to do,
There's much more to do for you,
So with prayers and my tears,
I will be attending you.

In spite of all the disappointments,
And repeated broken promises,
Can a mother's tender care,
Cease towards the child she bears.

In place of nothing else to do,
There is much more to do for you,
So with prayers and my heart,
I will be attending you.

You are one of my own,
Out of one womb grown,
I will not turn my back and hide,
Instead, I am ready to pray by your side.

In place of nothing else to do,
There's much more to do for you,
So with prayers on my knees,
I will be attending you.

The heart so hurt, will overflow,
Mind embroiled, no room to grow.
But with prayers released to realize,
Will hasten time to recognize.

I won't give up or cast no lot!
Won't let fear make me forget!
Will not surrender up my task!
For the child, I bear is still my cause.

In place of nothing else to do,
There's much more to do for you,
So with prayers unto my God,
I will be attending you.

Author: Marjorie E. Edwards
Created: November 6, 2010

Dedicated to all the Mothers

THE LAST TIME THAT YOU PRAYED

When was the last time that you prayed?
Did you talk to Him about your problems today?
Did you kneel upon your knees however, anyway?
So when was the last time that you prayed?

In our lives, there are many trials be,
We think all alone we can handle the turmoil be,
But when those forces repel our human strength,
That's when self knows that it's time to be renewed.

This world and what it offers in display,
So many choices we tend to partake in along the way,
But that void will only be fulfilled without delay,
If the Savior within our hearts comes to stay.

To many a man, sometimes we think all is gone,
For me, there will never be another chance,
But the Almighty, unto us a son, he was born,
To give the victory of taking us back in his arms.

Author: Marjorie E. Edwards
Created: January 11, 2011

WHAT PRAYER CAN DO

What prayer can do?
You may have no clue!
What our God will do?
He will do it all for you!

As I stand here today,
All my fears have all entered,
My testimony will reveal the pain,
I've been through over and over again.

I am not ashamed,
To tell you the comfort I gained,
From calling out to 'Him' in pain,
And He took my agony refrained!

I called out to Him in prayer!
Like there was no tomorrow,
A mother who felt the pain,
And my God delivers again!

What prayer can do?
You may have no clue!
Yes, our God will do.
Do it all, all for you!

Author: Marjorie E. Edwards
Created: October 1, 2011

WHY GOD CREATED YOU

Why God created you?
All for the reason of relating you,
He knows that you could not do without,
Fellowship in unity when it comes about.

Why God created you?
Is to put your talents in use,
In as much as not to be abused,
The spirit of sharing to enthuse.

Why God created you?
I know this for a fact!
Among the many 'He' had selected,
The choice is yours of duty to protect.

Why God created you?
Is to keep the dream alive,
And from others must not deprive,
But share and nurture vision to strive.

Why God created you?
In a world to breathe and be free,
To give a helping hand and not to flee,
From the life, He created for you and for me.

Author: Marjorie E. Edwards
Created: November 24, 2011

GRATIFICATION

AT THE DAWN OF DAY

At the new dawn and the light of the day,
When the twilight clouds, hastily steal away,
And the rising sun slowly appears with vigor to share,
Within the valleys deep, its warmth and blazing stare!

Echoes of pounding feet, strolling and striding,
Sounds of moving vehicles, rolling cautiously by,
When the pigeons get frightened and flutter away,
And the ducks squat still on the green grassy sway.

Mr. Squirrel, crunches as he partakes of the thrills,
From the seeds that were laid down to steal,
While the snail releases its unstressed array,
As we walk by and bid it safe on its way .

When the grass unleashes its verdant growth,
As the sprinklers toss their refreshing shout!
The ducklings splash in the silence deep!
Upon the pond awakened from its nocturnal sleep.

Here comes all, ready to work and willing to treat,
When the music of activities begins for everyone to compete,
A promising day, with all the surprises to display,
At the new dawn and the light of the day.

Author: Marjorie E. Edwards
Created: June 5, 2010

GLAD WE ARE HERE

Today we create yet another era,
Since the days we learn to count our zeros,
With a hearty smile, and all the gratitude,
The same students of 'Martin School.'

It all goes back to the seventies,
When our young minds mold with securities,
Reassured with the power of prosperity,
From the golden hands of Mistelle, and we glad we are here!

Glad she is here all by our side,
Glad she is here all for this ride,
Glad she is here, oh let us sit beside,
We are glad to be here.

We came from the old hilltop school,
So young together with the learning tool,
We were the many to carry out its rule,
With the caring teachers of 'Martin School.'

We had devotions and dismissals then;
We clasped our hands, and we count to ten,
Said our prayers with one eye opened,
Just to see where our teacher stands.

Glad we're here, by each other's side,
Glad we're here, all for this ride,
Glad we're here, oh let us sit beside,
We are glad to be here.

Remember the days when we shared suck, suck,
Eat bulla cakes and jumped hopscotch,
We played some cricket with the hard board bat,
And the guys, they were so hot.

We climbed the hills and slid with grace,
Thumped the ball and stopped on base,
Relished our lunches with all the waste,
At the sound of the bell, we'd be in haste.

Glad we're here, by each other's side,
Glad we're here, all for this ride,
Glad we're here, oh let us sit beside,
We are glad to be here.

Nutri -buns and the milk power mix,
Healthy portions each day all fixed,
Rice and bulgur with the curry chicken meat,
Until today, we keep it upbeat.

Our teachers from our noise, left with ringing ears,
For us, that's what they did endure,
And we thank them for all those devoted years,
To train us and send us for this world explore.

Glad we're here, by each other's side,
Glad we're here, all for this ride,
Glad we're here, oh let us sit beside,
We are glad to be here.

Then came the time with graduation stress,
Wishing each other our endeavors best,
Most of us didn't want to leave at all,
From the bonding seal, we have with all, that's why we are here.

We ran a mile around the school,
With our little skirts going flip, flop, flop,
P. E. exercises were all in place,
Gosh! Those were the good, golden days.

So, were glad we are here by each other's side,
Glad we are here, all for this ride,
Glad we're here, oh let us sit beside,
We're glad to be here.

Author: Marjorie E. Edwards
Created: January 25, 2011

Martin School Reunion. July 30, 2011

HE DID IT ANYWAY

It was just an evening going out,
When he called to give me a shout!
And then I waited on the time,
To say it out aloud,
And he did it, he did it anyway.

Then I put on mi cultural style,
And then I said it out with pride,
When I finished mi verses pile,
That man on your radio inside,
And he did it, he did it anyway.

He didn't call to ask for money,
Because he knew, I didn't have any,
He knew the gifts I have, been many,
When I told him sometimes, I may,
And he did it, he did it anyway.

And with the heart of a lion,
I know he is the man,
Who certainly makes entire plans,
To care for everyone,
And he did it, he did it anyway.

Will God's blessing be on him?
To take him through this land,
And I'm sure, he'll understand,
My gratitude today,
Yes, he did it, he did it anyway.

Author: Marjorie E. Edwards
Created: July 18, 2011

MORNING'S LAUGHTER

Happy sounds of emotional glee,
Interrupts the silence of the morning's free,
A joke from someone else in tone to share,
Echoing sounds of laughter everywhere.
On any given day, it is a great starter,
Sounds of the morning's laughter!

Laughter that makes "all eyes turn,"
With the heart, just ready to discern,
With all ears intending to learn,
What's the excitement to earn?
On any given day, it is a great starter,
Sounds of the morning's laughter!

Jingling sounds of the laughing humor,
Auditions the interest of the intenders,
With a wink, we all get in tone to stare,
From a chuckle to a jiggle in prone to share,
On any given day, it is a great starter,
Sounds of the morning's laughter!

The invigorating savor of instantaneous dip,
Encouraging task to take another sip,
An exuberant mood to get all in to stay,
Relaxing sway to assist throughout the day;
I tell you, on any given day, it is a great starter,
The melodies of the morning's laughter!

Author: Marjorie E. Edwards
Created: February 26, 2011

OUR ISLAND HOME

We share this paradise where lies our island home,
Where the moon shines bright, and the sun is known,
To fortify the authentic taste of all that nature owns,
And the fields stay green from the showering rain.

Where the radiant coats of clouds hover and protect,
A nation so fortunate with blessings and talents select,
With its rich terrains of beautiful, mountainous slopes,
And the skyline shores of our horizontal hopes.

Rivers, streams, and tributaries with cascading flows,
Where the rocks harbor and the fishes bestow,
Decorate the countryside with a slithering glow,
To the enchanting sounds of nature's melody.

Oh! The land of sugar cane and strong white rum,
Flavors of cultured spices, we could never undo,
Our productive soils, with copious crops compare,
Uphold its values for all to share.

Land of Caribbean bliss, love, peace, and harmony,
Music of soul stirring blues and redemption stories,
Spiraling far and wide, magnifying the hearts and souls,
Of all who've sailed our shores and climbed our mountain slopes.

When the time announces and the roosters pronounce,
For all to put their shoulders to the wheel,
To share the sun and commit together in fun,
Securing the legacy of our long last promises.

Jamaica! Land of magnificent beauty so rare!
Altitude of grace, comfort, and pleasures all fair,
Majestic skies of illuminant blue,
A paradise well treasured and not only to a few.

Author: Marjorie E. Edwards
Created: July 18, 2009

A Salute to our people, sons and daughters of the Carriblue Island of Jamaica
For the passionate and unconditional love, I have for the land of my birth.

The Cabarita Island in Port Maria. Saint Mary, Jamaica W. 1.

OUT OF A MILLION LOVES

Out of a million loves, He chooses me,
And places me in this world to beam.
Out of a trillion loves, He gave us this chance,
From a trillion journeys, He calls us to dance!

A brain, He gave us to prepare,
A heart, to all we ought to share,
He gave willing hands to help,
And feet that guide to make each step.

In our heart, He places His undying love,
That same God, wherever, way up above!
Within that new heart 'He' structured,
Enough to fulfill and secure our desires.

In our mother's womb a place He designs,
He blesses her with love secure and pure.
In richness, in beauty, all favors to shine,
He provides the will for her to endure.

His unique creation, His authoritative power,
Deem the rights to all His created treasure,
O love of life, preciously ordained to us as we are,
Out of a trillion who journey, He selected us wide and far!

"The gift of life is beautiful."

Author: Marjorie E. Edwards
Created: October 20, 2011

REUNION DEDICATION

Dearest family,
Have we ever imagined,
What it would be like,
To see each other's happy smiling faces again?

To recognize we are here,
From the earliest days, we expected to last,
A past that is filled with all the memories,
Most certainly, again we would like to relive.

Tonight we are here,
Thanking God for his marvelous care,
And not only that,
We have Mr. and Mrs. Haughton here, in fact!

Our sheriff, who maintained her role,
To help us focus on our imminent goals,
She taught that everyone has a purpose,
Stay awake and go quench your compelling thirst!

And as she stood in front of the classroom,
Of her young attentive eager believers,
With poised posture and a chalk in hand,
There was no exception from any receivers.

"The heights by great men reached and kept,
Were not attained by sudden flight,
But they, while their companions slept,
Were toiling upwards through the night."

We didn't understand much then,
But today, we realize back then were no playpen,
We had all the support at 'Martin School,'
Where we were armored with the powerful learning tool.

So many memories,
And so many notable years,
It seems like yesterday,
There is nothing that can fade it away!

Memories of secret silent crushes,
Fallen in love and creating different blushes,
Finding fault with others faces and noses,
But at no time, had we ever on each other imposed.

Today, I take the greatest pleasure,
To you, I unfold some of our festive memories,
For the first time, to the first people right here,
The memories come in sweet melody!

Author: Marjorie E. Edwards
Created: July 23, 2011

Martin School Reunion. July 30th, 2011

THE MUSIC OF THE OCEAN

The infinite ocean reaching far and wide,
Seemingly secured by the horizontal sky,
Music drifting yonder to each and every side,
To the dancing melody of the oceanic tide.

Savor of the briny sea breeze,
Releases its flavor for all to please,
Shoals of dancing fishes in perfect encore,
On the ocean floor, swimming along the shore.

Mounting forces of splashing waves all airborne!
Claim its ruler ship, its territory in its home zone,
Weeds of greenish brown bouncing about and within;
Scattering on the shore, the cool liquid mineral brings.

Slapping waters so deep, rock in motion of intensity,
Comforting sand, all laid to release its soothing energy,
And as the sun dims its daily source of natural chemistry,
The night's silence reveals the task of the sea in harmony.

A meeting place of lovers walking in the sand,
A privilege from the ocean brought to everyone,
Whether a wanderer, or a sailor with whatever stands,
The music of the ocean, its melody sings a special song.

Author: Marjorie E. Edwards
Created: August 29, 2011

Sunset on the beach. Montego Bay, Jamaica W.I.

48

THE MOON AND I

Far from the distance in the eastern sky,
Glows the incandescent moon on high!
From where that charming beauty lies,
Tonight it will be just the moon and I.

That glistening light among the trees,
Its radiance for the entire world to see,
Shining bright to offer its visionary ride,
Upon this ideal thought, it will be just the moon and I.

Wow! What a vibrant and notable sight,
It will surely claim the focus of this night!
With its distinguishing and attractive features,
The illumination nurtures with just the moon and I.

The moon in all its sparkling transparency,
Draws the attention in ushering tendency,
I watched as it revealed its melody nigh,
In utterly comfort with just the moon and I.

At some point, I missed its light,
But that moon just kept me all in sight.
Quite some distance now and it is still on my right,
An infinite memory just between the moon and I.

I felt real safe driving with the moon at nights,
No distraction from its nocturnal might,
Yet, it will be somewhere else in a little while,
It's just not enough time, for the moon and I.

What I have seen is fulfillment to include,
From the recall, nothing will ever be secluded,
Within my mind, made so rich to comply,
To that extra thrust just between the moon and I.

Many full moons, I have seen over the years,
But each time it is different from the last,
Time refines with appreciation, more to care,
Next time the moon and I, a little longer will spare.

Author: Marjorie E. Edwards
Created: March 7, 2011

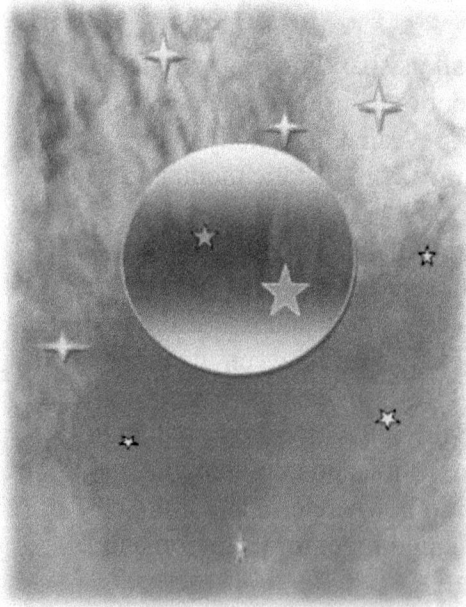

THE PALMS IN BLOOM

Standing tall with grace and beauty,
Enchanting height of nature's purity,
Captivating sight of exploring scenery,
Spectacular view, all palms in bloom.

Fresh and friendly, yellow and white décor,
Fragrance of rich aroma ready to explore,
Shredded buds expelled in merger allure,
From the palm trees, high and so secure.

When the gardeners stride within the gates,
And the day finishes its shaving wastes,
The splendor and fulsome luster ends,
From the trees lost and fading spent.

In the calmness of the night's tranquil rest,
Limbs lift high with all their beauty to last,
Yellow bellflowers with their melodies bring,
The intriguing palms dancing with the wind.

God's nature in abundance with purity restores,
The gift of beauty in greatness ensures.
Just can't keep a flourishing tree down,
What a spectacular view, the palms in full bloom.

Author: Marjorie E. Edwards
Created: June 17, 2010

WHEN I LOOK AT YOU

When I look at you,
I see your real entity,
Of perfection, and not without,
The reason for true integrity,
You capture my thoughts with total honesty.

When I look at you,
And with choices of all the privileges I have,
When you have to make all the sacrifices,
Of showing how fortunate I am,
Yet I complain about everything I can.

When I look at you,
I know there's a reason why you came.
To show us how to appreciate life's game,
To be humble and share this earthly fame,
To be grateful for everything just the same.

When I look at you,
I see dreams being accomplished,
Visions implemented to embellish,
Not conquered with substantial wishes,
But satisfied with principles of humble beliefs.

When I look at you,
Working for the reason to educate,
To share in earnest for others to emulate,
In every way, surmounted with altitude,
With a purpose to procure the cause in gratitude.

When I look at you,
We have a lot to do,
Not with pride and jealousy,
But with humility and authenticity,
The true meaning of stewardships.

Author: Marjorie E. Edwards
Created: November 17, 2011

Humility
Authenticity
Stewardships

DON'T NEED ANYONE BREAKING

I don't need anyone breaking my heart,
Even though right now, it's just a new start,
But sometimes, you don't even know,
When it comes for real, you've got to take it slow.

Said true love does not come easily,
Don't dare to play with stupidity,
Exercise it with pure honesty,
When found, it will be your true destiny.

You put your point in for a review,
Come to share and try to renew,
That broken heart that fell all apart,
O gives a chance to heal the broken heart.

I come to know if you are true,
In references of all my past blues,
Today you told me, you are one to renew;
You don't even know what I've been through!

Reserve a task to change my mind,
You hear that word often all the time,
And if I see where you are genuine,
Then of course you may get the chance!

Author: Marjorie E. Edwards
Created: January 18, 2011

HE TOOK THE TIME OUT

You keep on putting him off,
Boy, how much that must have hurt!
That wall you keep on building up,
Not to get him in, another one to slip!

If you keep on saying no,
Then he'll have no choice but to go.
You keep on playing hard,
Then he won't give you his guard!

A man needs his special attention,
Not to say more to mention,
If he took the time out to say "Hi,"
Then don't waste the time to say "Goodbye!"

You keep on staying low,
With his heart, he wants to show,
His wish that you would not be that darn slow!
You, he adores and wants to tell you all he knows.

Share your aim,
Appreciate the game,
Reach out to him and claim,
Become his heir, and accept his fame.

A joy to have and behold,
It is a comfort, more than gold,
If he took the time out to say "Hi,"
Then don't waste the time to say "Goodbye!"

Author: Marjorie E. Edwards
Created: October 15, 2011

IF YOU KNOW YOU LOVE HER

If you know you love her,
Then why so shy to tell her?
She might be waiting, for that little aid,
To show how hard she's to persuade.

If you know you love him,
Then why be too proud to tell him?
He might be waiting, for that little charm,
To fall straight into your arms.

If you know you are in wanting,
Then why won't you apply?
There might be waiting, for you that little chance,
To fully make your advance.

If you know you are in needing,
Then, why won't you surrender?
There might be waiting, for you such a game,
To get all wild and untamed.

So, come on, give it a try!
Listen to your own silent cry,
Somehow, someway you'll decide,
Just slow down and keep it satisfied.

Author: Marjorie E. Edwards
Created: July, 2009

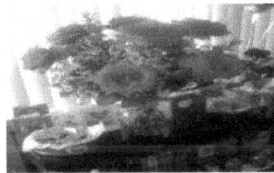

IN A MAN'S WORLD

Too much, too little, doesn't really matter,
Every time he sees her, his comforter,
His dreams no exception to forfeiture,
In a man's world, it's all about his new girl.

Comes what may, he gives to analyze,
Even though, sometimes she may criticize,
Her hopes and dreams all will be realized,
In that man's world, it's all about his precious girl.

Her beauty he uses to comfort the same,
And hopes, that it continues on again and again,
That their hearts grew to savor the love it rained,
Because, in a man's world, it's all about his only girl.

He protects and preserves while keeping his guard,
Be anxious when others prompt or likely to interfere,
With that passion, he created proudly for himself to last,
In that man's world, nothing matters but his beautiful girl.

Author: Marjorie E. Edwards
Created: September 28, 2011

I WISH YOU WERE HERE

Away from you, it is quite some distance,
I am here, and you are out there,
But, our hearts claimed in such an instance,
And you wish I was there.

You wish I were there, to fill your sight,
Wish I were there, just to talk up tight,
Wish I were there, it would be alright,
Oh! Oh! Oh! Oh! You wish I were there.

We talked for hours, on topics all crazy,
I'm your love, your queen, and your lady,
We talked over time, with diligent care,
You are my future, my dreams, and my baby,
And Oh! Oh! Oh! Oh! You wish I were there.

My picture I shared with you by text,
You assured me, that I'm still your best,
Your picture, I placed upon my desk,
Baby, you are the best!

Said, I deserve the best there is,
From a man like you to a woman like me,
To me, you are convincible,
When I'm to you, irresistible
And Oh! Oh! Oh! Oh, I wish you were here.

Wish you were here, to fill my sight,
Wish you were here, just to talk up tight,
Wish you were here, it would be alright,
Oh! Oh! Oh! Oh! Oh! I wish you were here.

Author: Marjorie E. Edwards
Created: January 17, 2011

I Miss You.
Come back soon.

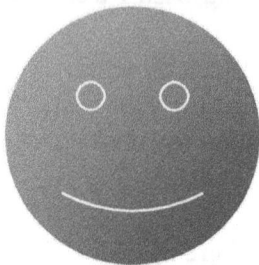

LETTER TO MY VALENTINE

Dearest valentine to be,
Bring your world to share with me,
That special love that sets me free,
From the lost and wounded me.

All this time, I was in a phase,
When your heart so full of grace,
Snapped away all the darken plight,
And placed me in your heart of light.

They say, love doesn't come easily,
But I'm not sure, how hard that be,
Real love sometimes feels like fantasy,
But it all depends on you and me.

You are the charmer of this night,
Share with me your love so delight,
Take me yonder up to the skies,
And show me where the stars in silhouette lie.

Upon the clouds, we'll cushion hide,
Without the least of selfish pride,
For to you, my love, I'll give my all,
Because you are my valentine!

Then our love shall forever endure,
Perfect ways to settle more,
All the sunlight from our hearts,
Will shine in us forevermore.

Sincerely,
Your dearest valentine!

Author: Marjorie E. Edwards
Created: January 3, 2011

To My Valentine With Love

LOVE IS ALL I'VE GOT FOR NOW

Your birthday's coming, and darling I know,
You ask what I'm giving, but I don't even know.
I'd like to make some plans while holding your hands,
But love is all I've got for now!

I'd like to get a boat that sails in the sand,
I'd like to take you away to a foreign land,
I'd like to do a lot, don't even know how,
But baby, love is all I've got for now!

I'd like to dress up, and perform like a clown,
Doing funny tricks jumping up and down,
I'd like to keep you smiling without a frown,
Honey, love is all I've got for now!

I'd like to fix you a meal with exotic tastes,
Putting that special smile upon your face,
And waiting on you without any haste,
Real love is all I've got for now!

I'd like to get a pole and dance that special role,
I'd like to sure fit, and work all my goals,
I'd like to polish and keep you shining like gold,
My darling, love is all I got for now!

Author: Marjorie E. Edwards
Created: July 18th, 2011

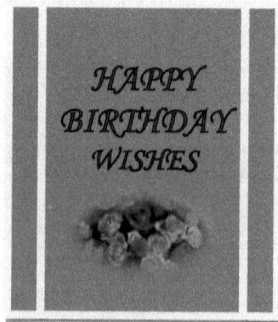

HAPPY
BIRTHDAY
WISHES

LOVE IS ONE THING

If you think you feel it,
Might as well you give it,
And if you think you need it,
It is something we can't do without!

Love is what we can't do without!
If you know you believe it,
Why not give it all you got?
Love is one thing we can't do without!

Sometimes love doesn't come so easily,
But when you're sure you've found it,
Get out there and claim it,
Put the will to show how far it will go!

In these times the best thing to do,
Is to love and be happy,
Lose the stress that comes with anxiety,
And be that peace to refresh the society.

Take the time to receive,
And make the time to give,
Uphold those values to contain,
One wish that will ever come through.

Author: Marjorie E. Edwards
Created: October 31, 2011

SAID YOU CAME TO SHARE

Said you came to share with me.
True love together we will be,
When you showed how much you cared,
My heart you stole, in depth to share.

With all my love, I will give!
'Cause I will always receive,
For to you, I have to be honest,
Your true love has earned my promise.

With all the languages of sincerity,
There is all the time to compromise,
And the comforting securities,
There is no pretense while we reside.

With all my heart, I'll share,
And I will always be near,
For to you, I have to be honest,
Your true love has earned my promise.

Yes, we need each other for shelter,
To help us through this trying time,
So, right here we are all that matters;
'Cause our love will never falter.

With all my life, I'll share,
'Cause, I know you will take care
For to you, I have to be honest,
Your true love has earned my promise.

Author: Marjorie E. Edwards
Created: July 10, 2010

THERE WAS A LONELY HEART

There was a lonely heart,
Who sought a cheerful mind,
So he asked to be her friend,
With all intentions to the end.

She said, "Don't you dare pretend!
There is no joy from your intent,
Turn your head the other way!
And find yourself another heart to stay!"

With a smile upon his face,
And outstretched hands in place,
He said, "I have already claimed your heart,
And that's where I want to start."

Then she looked straight into his eyes,
And saw no fear from any lies,
Then answered, "I'll be your friend
'Cause, you just won my heart again!"

Then together in hands and heart,
Allow their peace with them abide,
And with such standards set on high,
Their future prepared with all its worth resides.

Author: Marjorie E. Edwards
Created: September 20, 2010

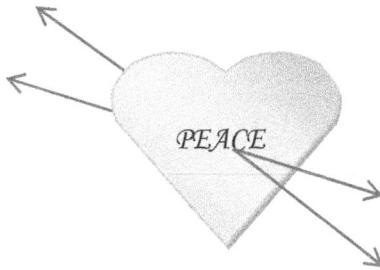

PEACE

THE THRILLS TO REIGN AGAIN

Man and woman are like night and day,
However, they communicate in unique ways,
Some say, It's the Hoe that finds its stick,
Others say, Cho, all a dem too darn slick!

Two friends in love are bound to share,
Every reason of how much they do care,
But sometimes sudden distractions appear,
Then anxieties materialize to chilling fears!

For love and security, each must be willing,
To fortify the charisma in giving and receiving,
Sharing values that support in all, as much
To secure the need of that long-lasting trust.

Time spent together helps to share even more,
Embracing ideas and making up to the score,
Discovering ways, even with the coldest to endure,
With humble passion, and much patience to implore.

Sensitivity in thoughts and all actions,
Will resolve issues of concern with positive expectations,
Ensure the togetherness with more appreciation,
And persuade the integrity to the fullest satisfaction.

To each, give sincerely all that there is to share,
Never be in doubt nor surrender to any fear,
Life can be committed with so much more to gain,
When the thrill surfaces to reign again.

Author: Marjorie E. Edwards
Created: April 2009

68

TO CARESS

Caress and hold me comfortably and secure,
With everything to give and much more,
The kindness of your tender stroke,
With the apparent intent to provoke.

Sensual touch as gentle to squeeze,
Sweet emotions, it stirs to tease,
Vigorous attractions in volume releases,
The color of love, so synchronizing it pleases.

Caress and hold me tight tonight,
Shower me with the power of your might,
Let me release this stress and the pain,
Within your embrace of comfort to entertain.

Oh! Help me to think highly, and not in vain,
My thoughts all to you so I will retain,
Caress and hold me comfortably and secure,
Give me all you've stored, and I will endure.

My joy and leisure alluringly propose,
I will not refuse anything I suppose,
Caress and hold me comfortably and secure,
My life, my dreams to you I will give more.

Author: Marjorie Edwards
Created: November 23, 2011

WISH YOU HADN'T FALLEN

In the ecstasy, of sweet Lo-lo byes,
There come periods of saying goodbyes,
So, never give up my dear,
To your young life, it's all unfair,
Just because you wished, you hadn't fallen in love.

No one said, it's a game played all fair,
To you, my dear, life must declare,
But it's better you say, you wish you hadn't,
Than to say, you wish you would,
Just because you wished, you hadn't fallen in love.

Please don't give up my dear,
Be beautiful in someone else's care,
If he is now gone,
To you, he never did belong,
Just because you wished, you hadn't fallen in love.

Be strong, my friend!
Another will come again!
And this time, you will know,
There will always be more room to grow,
Just because you wished, you hadn't fallen in love

Oh, open up your heart, my child!
I know you are all hurting inside,
No, no, do not hide your only life away!
The true love, someday will come to stay,
Just because you wished, you hadn't fallen in love.

Author: Marjorie E. Edwards
Created: March 23, 2011

70

ENCOURAGEMENT AND MOTIVATION

A FRIEND WITHIN MY PEN

With my pen, I will befriend,
A forever friend to the end,
Ready to give and showers its ink,
On paper, it glides and helps me to think.

My friend, my pen,
A forever friend to the end,
As long as God continues to send,
Creative ideas for me to comprehend.

I found a friend within my pen,
A forever friend to the very end,
To the windows of the souls I plea,
Words of comfort all in dynamic glee.

I found a friend within my pen,
A forever friend, all to the end,
Willingly sparing the time to participate,
Destine stories to inspire and associate.

I found a friend within my pen,
Oh, written words focused with intent,
Come alive in many ways to generate,
Zeal to last, for more than a moment's gaze!

Author: Marjorie E. Edwards
Created: October 2, 2011

I Found a friend within my pen

AS I LOOK THROUGH MY WINDOW

As I look through my window,
I saw a bright new beginning.
The reality of the morning's blessing,
Best of all, existing in perfect grandeur.

I reckoned back to the delay of the yesterdays,
Thinking about the future, and tomorrow task,
All hopes of vision secure the now presence in loom,
Guiding into the future, where hence, light cometh soon.

I will have the wind to help me fly!
There will be more than wings for me to try!
I will accomplish my goals, whatever comes nigh,
Because my mind is set, and I know the reason why.

Author: Marjorie E Edwards
Created: August 29, 2011

AS SILENT AS THE NIGHT

As silent as the night seems,
There is a musical stream,
Though the darkness is all there,
The shadow sends me no fear.

I found peace in this tranquil night,
The content of this gestural sight,
A peace all clear to focus in getting,
A restful night ahead in humble setting.

Preparing for the night, here goes,
In comfort, with no worry to know,
My relaxing zone so tenderly eases,
As the melody, of the soothing music teases.

On my pillow rest my head to go,
Finding that spot in colorful glow,
Listening, as the streaming music flows,
Accompanying each breath as it blows.

Another chore to go,
The nightly journey plows,
Eyes slowly closed as far as I can remember,
Off to sleep in soothing and curing slumber.

My mind rests and certainly grows
During my sleep, there all it shows,
From the night's silence, comes the daylight's serene,
Awaken from my dream to the morning's sunbeam.

Author: Marjorie E. Edwards
Created: November 6, 2011

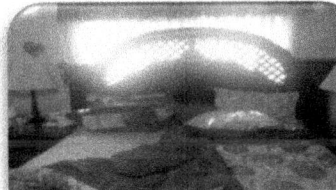

BEFORE I GO

Before I go, I will have to care for you,
Before I go, there is a lot I have to do,
Will you give me a little chance?
For me to render my assistance.

I need time to do it all for you,
Putting it off again will never do
You any good this time to stay,
In this mood, for the rest of the day.

I will take special care to render to you,
All the basics coming from me to you,
To make you refreshed and renewed
I will even apply a session of exercise too.

So here we start,
And I'll play my part,
And yours is to supply,
The will, which together, we will apply.

Up, I'll help you to sit,
Then your shoes I'll try to fit,
And for you to stand,
I will lend you my hand.

Then, while, we walk,
We'll have a little talk,
About life, all that you can remember,
Of which, you are such an honorable member.

I'm truly enjoying each day,
Staying here, to help you in every way.
And pray that when my time is at hand,
God will send an angel to help me understand.

Author: Marjorie E. Edwards
Created: December 28, 2010

BELIEVING IN YOU

Do you believe in you?
Well I do too, and I must tell you,
First things come firstly due,
You have to believe in you.

Maybe you are not so much of a strong effort,
So these words will be here for your support,
To release the stress of feeling all too timid,
In assurance, you do have the right to forbid.

You have been provided with the will,
But you have to channel the way,
Go for it! Never mind the potential bill,
Your better chance starts today!

Point your aims and golden aspirations,
Towards the areas of destined directions.
Doesn't matter if on the first time you fail,
Life comes with more chances to prevail.

Reach for the stars to the height of the skies!
The clouds are all there for a worthy bumpy ride,
With providential guidance already placed at your side,
The prize awaits you yonder, wherever your destiny lies.

Author: Marjorie E. Edwards
Created March 2, 2011

CAN'T GIVE UP NOW

Some friends told me, there has to be a way,
But it is so frustrating to start and be persistent to stay,
With a business too long, five years for a decent profit,
Money been spent to maintain the same topic,
Can't give up now, I have got to find a way,
Tomorrow is always another day!

Times get so hard, you just want to drop it!
However, already started, much harder to stop it!
I know time to come; there'll be some gain,
But right now, it is causing me too much pain!
Nevertheless, I cannot give up now; it is a long way to go
Can't give up now, that is all I know!

The heart is willing, but the intent is weak,
When the negative forces try to pull me off my feet,
And silence me in battle of defeat,
I worked too hard, accomplishments almost complete!
Can't give up now, I have to find a new course!
Can't give up now, have to fight this interminable force!

I will not give up; it is my ambition to stay!
I have no time to waste or to play!
Can't give up now, my cake is almost finished baking,
Can't give up, I have to be ready to claim my taking,
Can't survive with thoughts being borrowed;
I am going to look up, and pray for all my tomorrows.

Author: Marjorie E. Edwards
Created: December 30, 2010

DECEPTION

Oh! From the deception,
Comes all the rejections,
Making one becoming cold,
Within their reachable goal.

Deception, true meaning of dishonesty,
Comes with selfishness in its entirety,
One should never be amused,
From this unkind, and inferior ruse.

People are different,
And each heart is separate,
That simply means that the way one feels,
The other does not systematically yield!

If you say, I'm ugly,
If you say, I'm fat,
I won't believe you,
Because I'm none of that!

True meaning of love,
Encourages and forgive.
But it's difficult to move forward,
With the burdensome strains of thinking backwards.

Author: Marjorie E. Edwards
Created: December 5, 2011

INSECURITY

Insecurity is what's killing you!
Insecurity, it is not good for you,
Been down and out, mountains all about,
Because of those trifling insecurities.

Ambitions planned with all the dreams,
Would reach far and wide for all it seems,
Ensures with all the inspirational safety,
Now you're left in doubt because of insecurity

Been surrounded by empty theories,
Cannot be content in your own sanctuary!
Have no trust in others standing by you,
So mixed up because of impoverish realities!

Too empowered with silly precautions,
That strongly entices your application,
Your own defense creates you as a prisoner,
Insecurity compels you as your own tormentor.

Would you think I want to join your flock?
I know much better than that,
So, you can definitely take that all back,
Your insecurity made you such a mock!

I don't have to prove to you anything!
My sincerest role upholds me everything,
From deep within to my outward strength!
Security for me, is all it brings!

I share because I'd rather be true than be blue,
With enough blessings to supply me and for you,
Considering others as it multiplies in abundant view,
My duty remains in spite of your discouraging clue*!*

Don't hate me because of my generosity,
Deep down the best I can do for prosperity,
My attitude is endearing, sweet, and sophisticating,
Brought up rich, with integrity, and a high self-esteem mentality!

Author: Marjorie E. Edwards
Created: November 11, 2011

I WANT TO SHARE IN GIVING

I want to share in giving,
From all my stories told,
So give me all the reasons,
For me to inspire your soul.

I have to share in giving,
We all can have some fun,
Throughout the yearly season,
I will work from dusk till dawn.

For me to share in giving,
I will have to write my songs,
But we have to be willing,
To dance and sing along.

I must share in giving,
So let us sing it out,
Together we'll share in giving,
The spirit of joy to dance about.

Author: Marjorie E. Edwards
Created: September, 2008

I WISH I KNEW

I wish I knew what lies ahead in life,
Wouldn't you?
But, whatever I've known is already behind,
So true!

What lies yonder in suspense?
I have no clue,
But the attempt to start this journey,
Will all be in the queue.

I wish I knew what I'll find, will contend
My mind in view,
Then my heart will be satisfied,
And feel anew.

I hope I will find that path
To let me through,
And reach that height of joy
To share with you.

I pray that humility will
Content my zest,
Help me at every crossroad,
To pass each trial's test.

So, if I knew what lies ahead,
It would be comprehensible to know.
Therefore, my plans will be for me,
To be, the very, very best that I can be.

Author: Marjorie E. Edwards
Created: December 22, 2010

I WISH I HAD THE TIME

I wish I had the time to tell,
About the passion, in which I dwell,
The thoughts all cultivated in my head,
But the time will not avail itself instead.

Sometimes, time can be defined,
But, there are times when there is no time,
To reveal the facts carried in full detail,
About the passion, that enthuses to prevail.

Only if we have time,
Is the answer all the time,
Time to endorse the preliminaries,
And hope that it will be revealed in completeness.

Author: Marjorie E. Edwards
Created: November 24, 2011

Only
if
we have
enough time.

IT ALL DEPENDS ON YOU

It all depends on you,
Whatever you do, please always be true,
It may come someday to haunt you,
And in most cases, you may never see through.

Wherever you go,
All the courtesy to show,
Not only to those who need it to grow,
But, also to everyone whom you come to know.

Whatever you see,
With all the realities to be,
Your power of choice will secure your vision,
It all depends on the concept of your affirmative action.

Whatever you share,
Be positive and clear,
You never know who may be in need of a helping hand,
And your friendship may just be the perfect one.

Author: Marjorie E. Edwards
Created: March 1, 2011

THE DREAM I DREAMT

The dream I dreamt was all too real
The nightmare of terror all in detail,
Throughout my hazy nocturnal hell,
I could not find me a place to dwell.

Dreamt I walked the lonely path,
For comfort, I yearned to depart,
Up the hilly mountain, I could not sort,
In darkened path, no way to find a start.

Wire fences stored high above,
I gazed with fear, looking for love,
Lonely planes, no movement beside,
Wish I could find a place just to hide.

Crawled in spaces of dampened dust,
On hands and feet there all, I thrust,
Darkened tunnel all alone, one way to go,
Where yonder ahead, there was a dim of light.

Empowered by the revealing charm
Oh! Dim of light, out of danger's harm!
And, alas at the new daylight's dawn,
Found myself cuddled in my bed and barn.

Author: Marjorie E. Edwards
Created: August 2, 2011

NEVER LEFT WITHOUT

I am never left without,
A thought to write about,
When the stanzas are reviewed,
Another limerick starts anew.

I may have surprised your interest,
When you questioned, "How do I behold?"
But just like you, I'm well-blessed and impressed,
With the messages sent me from my soul.

Same way I received it, I have to give it,
Have to be keen on how to deliver it,
In order to portray the revealing image,
It must associate with the factual linkage.

I do not dwell on things that make me sad,
Wholesomely, my mind has to be all clear,
The mission is to inspire us all to be glad,
From the messages all submissively prepared.

My desire is to acclaim the smallest of things to God for praise,
The divine power of our individual and gifted intellect,
And hoping, that nothing will ever be erased,
From the selections sent for me all to illustrate.

How much do I appreciate life's beauty,
Makes me resonate in ode of gratifying duty,
From the thoughts, I am never left without,
When always there is a topic to write about.

Author: Marjorie E. Edwards
Created: February 22, 2011

OUR BRAIN

Our brain works all the time,
Even in our sleep, we call it a dream,
It balances to make us stay in line,
But sometimes, we tend to want to scream!

The power of our mental acumen,
Started out from the very beginning,
Even before getting our hands and toes,
Our brain tells us what we should know.

It all goes back to the gift of consciousness,
Our ingenious humor we share in awareness,
The reason why we were provided with this brain,
Is to apply our intelligence to remain.

With others, we'll share the use of our ingenious brain,
To benefit the joy in everything for us all to gain,
To resolve all the complicated issues on us thus pile,
Let us use it to make our lives happy and worthwhile.

Author. Marjorie E. Edwards
Created: January 1, 2011

Intellegence
Optimism Integrity
Empathy Gratitude
Happiness
Equality

89

ONLY YOU KNOW YOU

Only you know your testing times,
When life's pressure to you incline,
When you need to relax for just a while,
To renew the damaged spirit within you.

It is only you who can decide,
If you want to count stars or squares,
If you want to reach out and share,
Only you, you can spare.

At times, you want to stay alone,
All with that silence claimed to own,
Wish to have the reality take a break,
Which only you can make.

When that silence reveals its truth
From the loneliness of staying blue,
Then it is time to share your fruit,
With the prospects of refining you.

After you get that break to reset,
Then out the door in motion you will step,
To face more facts, of knowing yourself,
Because, only you know you.

Author: Marjorie E. Edwards
Created: December 23, 2010

SAVE THAT TEAR

Life is what you make it,
All depends on how you take it,
It comes with the good and the bad,
But it's your choice not to be sad.

The hurt that ripped inside,
Most times lingered and pushed aside,
We kept on hanging on,
It happened to everyone.

Signs show you will know,
Each message sent still flows,
Time spent with all the passing,
Left to gather strength in lasting.

Do not hanker to say:
It won't get better each day,
It's best for you to be aware,
Be wise to save that tear.

Author: Marjorie E. Edwards
Created: November 15, 2011

SOME DAY I WILL WRITE AGAIN

The pain had pass but the hurt contrast,
I still remember that dreaded task,
Creative thoughts on paper to last,
Intended flame, my scripted memories collapsed,
But someday, I will write again.

The ashes from those hated flames,
I stood helpless and watched in vain,
With steaming tears, from my eyes it drained
My hopes, my creations, that consuming pain,
But someday, I will write again.

Reading consoles my comfort,
But writing, I always depend on that,
Someone who's supposed to care and protect,
Took my first collections, smoked in black,
But someday, I will write again.

And when I do,
I will certainly make sure,
The benefits will all be insured,
To keep them within gated doors,
I know, someday, I will write again.

Had been a Poet from the early days,
But discouraged, suppressed, and dazed,
Question is why the relented laze?
Was just a matter of time to surface that faze,
It will come, that someday, I will write again.

Now the agony is all in the past,
But the memories they still last,
I cannot let go or depart,
It is still here, a place within my heart,
That will someday, help me to write again.

Author: Marjorie E. Edwards
Created: November 25, 2011

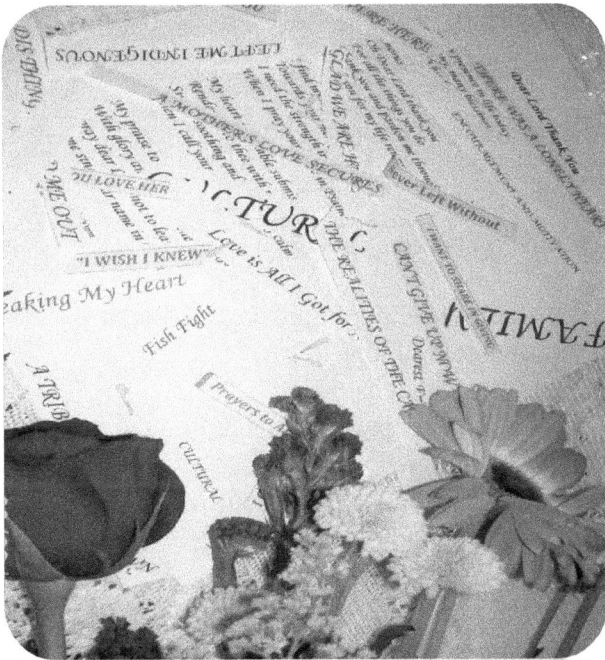

2011 HAD BEGUN

It was a thrilling time, with the festive fun,
That concluded yet another year to a milestone run,
To many, it was the worst; to others, new recourse,
When 2010 dipped deep into everyone's purse.

To those who have lost, it is time to believe and start anew,
For those who held on, keep the faith and struggle on,
Put out effort to succeed,
It is 2011, full time to proceed.

We have the power to choose this hour,
To help those in need to recover,
With Almighty God in charge,
In 2011 we must recharge.

The past is an experience, the future an anticipation,
Faith is the substance of things to get,
And the intentions of what to select,
In 2011, let's thrive to keep this in check.

To recognize our needs and suppress our wants,
Be vigilant and watch every qualm,
We stand tall with our heads held high,
When 2011 draws nigh.

Come let us with our dreams be realized,
Even if we are being criticized,
The past we'll use for a revision,
And let the creditors stay in their division,
When 2011 envisions.

Temptation to all will give its dose,
But we own the rights in many ways to oppose,
Not be distracted by negative drums go bang!
2011, will compel us to have that plan.

We are strong people with positive minds,
We will not allow just thoughts to pull us behind.
A strong nation that will certainly do well,
And 2011 comes with that will.

So let's have a productive year with great healthcare!
Treat each other well with lots of good cheer!
Continue to give God the glory for a brand new year,
And 2012 will come with its fair share.

Author: Marjorie E. Edwards
Created: December 12, 2010

"Happy New Year!"

THE VOICE THAT SATISFIES

The voice that sends a message,
While it surely teaches,
The voice that always gives the thrill,
And makes you want to keep still.

The voice with many special blessings,
That compels the need to listen,
That voice caught my attention at first,
And satisfyingly quenched my listening thirst.

Interesting thoughts that everyone seeks,
Remedy the mind and soul in all respect,
Travel far across on air to intensify our ego,
The soothing voice of that man inside your radio.

Receptive interest to informative and versed topics,
And the cool vibes in arrays of cultural prospects,
Inspiring, refreshing, humorous, and appealing,
We listen to his pleasant voice with true meaning.

Author: Marjorie E. Edwards
Created: November 6, 2010 – January 4, 2011
Dedicated to Rich Davis and the Rich Davis Show

The Man Inside Your Radio
www.themaninsideyourradio.com

Words From A Poet's Soul is proudly titled, exposed and endorsed by Rich Davis as part of the Rich Davis show on WLVJ1040am and WBZT1230am.This had made it into a household name during 2010-2012. Thanks to Rich Davis and the Rich Davis Show for this exposure, motivation and consistent support.

TIME

If time is the master,
And it does fly,
How can it be measured in motion,
When it is not at all literally seen?

To identify time with our dreams,
Time is the essence of all things,
Time is the acceptance of all intakes,
Time is the denouncement of all mistakes.

Time permits us to forgive,
And sometimes helps us to forget,
Time passes with its invisible fear,
But will allow the hope to spare.

Time dwells with our intelligence,
The potential of positive influence,
Time sometimes can be fearful,
When wasted with choices of regrets.

Time yield with the target of success,
Not only heals a broken heart in distress,
But gives a brand new start in whatever test,
And helps the willing achieve the very best.

Time is final,
Will not be in denial,
Time waits for no man,
Time enables us all to understand.

Time does not sleep,
All our secrets it keeps,
Time provides all the answers,
Because time will tell.

Author: Marjorie E. Edwards
Created: August 31, 2011

YOUR TALENT

Your talent is a gift,
And should not be suppressed,
By any circumstance come adrift,
But to use with earnest to invest.

Created talent used to influence,
Will build a mountain of intelligence,
Shared and impart structural self-worth,
Use to validate and maintain with support.

Not to be mistreated or depressed,
When it's been slammed and criticized,
But to share to acquire genuine interests,
Keep the guard up; to focus is to stay organized.

Author: Marjorie E. Edwards
Created: November 22, 2011

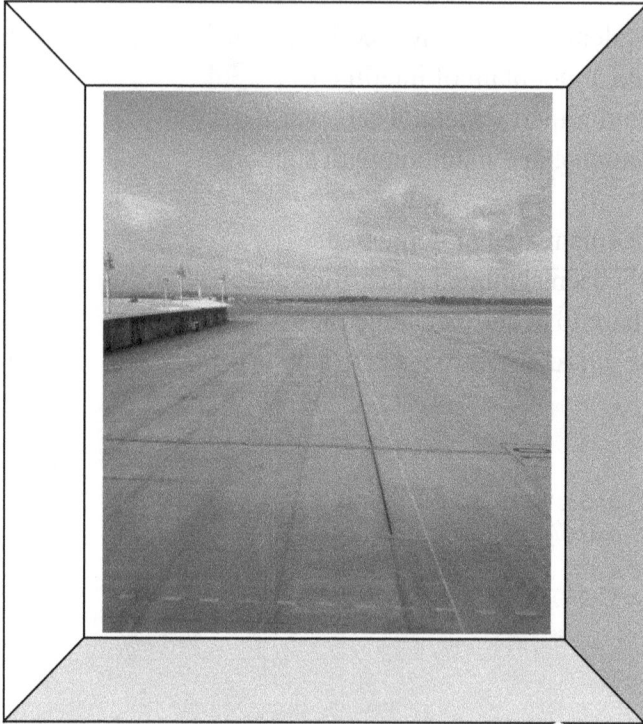

Upstairs shot
Norman Manley International Airport
Kingston, Jamaica W. I.

Cultural

AFTER SURGERY

Lawd mi God, wat a calamity,
Cyaan face up to dis catastrophe,
Wat a real big blow!
All a mi teet mi go show!

She asked mi if any cavity,
Mi tell har, 'Not in reality,'
She asked if dere is any chip,
Mi answer, 'Not even mi lip.'

Six months now, tings nuh right,
Mi teet not like dem used to bite,
Cyaan manage di food come within mi sight,
Mi fret, mi a go end up losing dis fight.

Start fi tink bout it now fi a while,
Not anymore fi join di modeling line,
Cyaan laugh out or open up mi mouth,
All a mi teet dem a wear all out.

Not even pon one side alone,
Mi cyaan eat mi potato pone,
No more desert an all a mi sweet treat,
After surgery lef mi teet all ill-treat.

Haffi tek any ting come forth,
Cyaan even cuss out di one Rupert,
Oh, mi teet dem a hurt,
It wuss dan giving birth!

"Mi cannot bite bone,
Without giving a groan,
Lawd, wat a come dung,
By dis it is well well known.

103

Cyaan eat dumpling,
Without dem slipping,
Cyaan drink cold beverage,
Mi teet dem gone pon edge!

Now dat mi teet dem a go,
Odda people dem a notice it too,
From mere concern, dem sen mi gift,
Packaged wid di "Chewing Bullet."

Author: Marjorie E. Edwards
Created: October 2, 2011

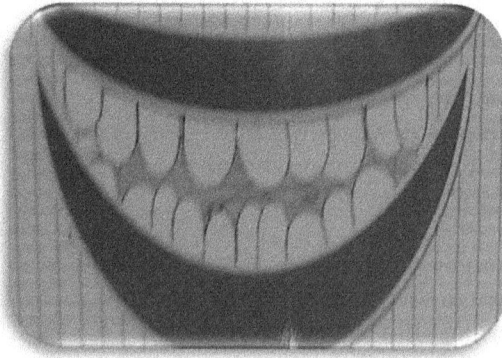

Mi

teet

dem

a go

A SIMPLE WORD TO DEFEND

Wid not enough hours at wuk an mi start fi worry,
Di time a get short, an mi haffi hurry.
Mi grab mi keys, mi bag, an mi blackberry,
Couldn't finish eating di lickle food mi curry.

Mi aim was to get to di site,
Tank God, mi reach pon time,
Mi drive wid a lot a care,
Fah di roads mi haffi share.

Mi get to wuk, all feeling fine,
Was ready fi join in line,
Yes, to wuk an not fi play,
She started wid all har twang'y way!

Mi nuh know wah or who she was seeing,
She speaks in language mi know nuttin bout,
All mi know is, it did sound mean,
An dat just stir up mi ego fi shout it out!

Mi set mi lip, an mi fix mi face,
Mi raises mi shoulder, an mi step in place,
Wid all di cultural style to display,
Mi just simply sey, "GWWWAAAYYY!"

She inhaled a heavy load,
Mi step back, fearing she going explode,
No doubt, mi was about to hit dat highway road,
But she cut har yeye, an den head towards di door.

Di fear was coming dung di more,
Mi peek fi mek sure she really went truu di door,
'Cause mi nuh trust no one wid dem rage!
Unexpectedly, dem tun round pon yuh well deranged.

Since dat day, hardly much ever been said,
But lately now it's just "Hi" an "By" instead,
All because mi mek mi way out to pretend,
With nuttin more dan just a simple word to defend.

Breathing right dat day was mi only way,
'Cause mi neva waan fi end up in an emergency stay,
Sometimes, yuh nuh need much to your defense,
Like mi, just use a simple word to defend!

Author: Marjorie E. Edwards
Created: June 27, 2008

DIS TING A TIAD MI OUT

"Dis ting a tiad mi out
Just by getting a working out,
From dis whole heap a walking,
Cyaan bother keep up wid di crude remarking."

Taking a stroll pon di wayside,
Wen 'im drove up beside,
Trying fi secure mi attention,
Wen to 'im, mi have no intention.

Wid 'im loud mouth, "Body looking good!"
Mi wish 'im wudda just galang as 'im should,
A sister cyaan walk fi get a little exercise,
Without "Bwoy Blue," stopping up to criticize?"

Wid 'im loud mouth, "Yuh must need a ride,"
"No Bwoy Blue, yuh nuh si mi a stride?"
Try fi pretend talking pon mi phone,
Fi 'im to be aware an lef mi alone.

'Im say, "Mi hear yuh call di 'B' word,"
Mi pretend as if to 'im mi neva heard.
'Im say, "Mi hear yuh said dat 'BB' word,"
Mi look straight dung pon di road.

'Im say, "Mi hear dat double 'BB' word,"
Mi still pretend as if to 'im not being heard.
'Im say, "Yuh can't talk, now yuh tun deaf?"
Now dis tells mi, tun straight back to mi lef.

'Im was a firing force,
Wat if dis thing come to di wuss?
Den it might really get out a hand,
'Cause mi nuh tek di ride inna 'im van.

Den mi hear di sound a tire screeching,
Wen 'im was on 'im way to 'im reaching,
Wid all di power away from dis living hell,
I u-turned straight back from dis homely spell.

Mi was breathing so short,
Haffi grab a seat an sidung real fast,
Di time mi tek fi walk dis lickle path,
Far away from hell bruk loose nearly star.

To be home was such a relief!
Didn't even badda fi tink wah tek place
Way out deh, almost cost mi sudden grief,
Wen 'im think mi answer was too bold face.

So sure dat mi could handle it,
But wen fear tek yuh over, yuh just lose it,
Some answers need not to repeat,
Almost find mi-self dung in a defeat!

Had no odda choice, but fi keep mi cool,
Tell mi-self mi had to stick to di safest rule,
Tried mi best fi defend to di very end,
When pride lef an end up round di bend!

Author: Marjorie E. Edwards
Created: July, 2009

FISH FIGHT

If yuh standing, please find a seat,
An if yuh sitting, do not retreat,
Listen an hear mi out real well,
An let mi tell yuh all bout mi ordeals.

Mi get a package from a fren,
Include some fishes straight from di sea,
Dat didn't go truu di regular trend,
Just to prove di difference in taste to mi.

Mi intention was to prepare dem fish,
For us to have a delicious dish,
Mi already had a piece a yellow yam,
Some scallion, thyme, pepper, an onion.

Have to get some more stuff in town,
Den return, an escovitch dem dung.
But dem darn fishes abuse mi so much,
Mi choose not fi go near dem wid a touch!

Mi wrapped dem well fi store dem away,
Really tink dat was enough fi di day,
Mi hands was in so much pain,
A fish dinner, dat evening, wasn't mi only claim!

Poor son come home wid hunger ache,
Looking fi a dinner to partake,
Rubbing 'im belly wid one hand,
An two crackers in di odda one.

So, you expect fi get a delicious dish,
Out a dem darn wicked fishes?
Yuh know wah dem fishes do to mi?
Wouldn't wish dat fi yuh wuss enemy!

'Im didn't know wat mi was talking bout,
How dem fishes attacked mi, it wasn't cool,
Dem pricked mi so hard,
Mi cussed dem bad, an even shout!

Mi friend called fi find out how it did wuk out,
If mi get di taste she tell mi about,
Mi figet di gratitude, an almost become rude!
No way could I ever enjoy dat cruel food!

She told mi, di scissors wudda been better,
To control dem, an keep dem all togedda.
Using a knife fi trim dem dung in di back,
Would only mek dem fight back an attack!

Well, di pain still lingers on fi now,
From di painful memory mi wi neva figet,
One ting mi know, is dat wen dat day come,
How mi going fi prepare, mi nuh even know yet.

Mm, yes, mi wi escovitch dem wid some juicy seasoning,
Di onion, pepper an vinegar appetizingly put dung,
Si wen mi sidung, an wid deese same hands,
Mi vengeful taste will all be satisfied from head to tail,
Afta all, it's a fish fight!!!!

Author: Marjorie E. Edwards
Created: July, 2010

JAMAICAN MAN

Special tings wid a Jamaican man,
God's gifted creative plan,
Wid unique strength an extreme abilities,
Dem so much in demand.

Wen it comes to di man, who fully understands,
How well needed to 'im a woman wid har hands,
He'll try in every way to supply her,
By becoming one of di best provider.

Not so much in playing other games,
Where some tink dat's where dem get all di fame,
But to wuk hard in all he can,
An to prove himself to be dat man.

Dem best motive to us is well-justify,
By giving all to satisfy,
An Oh, dem such great teasers,
An in di end, work out to be real pleasers.

Wen dem find you attractive, interesting, an enticing,
'Im made you special, to keep you smiling,
Wid dat sweet sprucely love chat,
Ladies, dem won't deprive you from dat.

Wen it comes to dem special interests,
Hard wuk, favorite food, an anyting else,
Dem leisure time well structurally planned,
Evolves around friends an family clans.

All good men for di perfect prize,
Di biggest hearts wid much comfort inside,
Culturally trained to invest an secure,
Fun an laughter enjoy di love much more.

Here comes now, fi di dancing contest,
Dem pick up foot an drop it dung di best,
Rhythmic rounds an exotic sound,
Make yuh crash out in deep snoring tone.

Special tings wid a Jamaican man,
God's gifted creative plan,
Up abroad or dung a yard,
Loving dem back is such a great reward.

Yes wi love wi Jamaican men,
God's gifted creative plan,
Up abroad or dung a yard,
Loving dem back is such a great reward.

Author: Marjorie E. Edwards
Created: June 19, 2007

LEF MI INDIGENOUS

Son, mi know yuh love yuh mama,
An mi dearly love yuh to,
But mi nuh waan di big life,
Wah mi cyaan afford fi live.

So lef mi indigenous,
An go back a yuh cottage,
Nuh come yah, come tell mi,
Wah fi throw out inna garbage.

Lef mi enamel plate,
Dem a inexpensive rate,
Put dung mi chip mug,
Mi nuh need no glass jug.

Lef mi grater,
Mi nuh need no blender,
Nuh tek mi wooden spoon,
Mi nuh need no mixer.

Lef mi iron pot,
Nuh fling dem inna dat,
Mi nuh need dat heavy knife,
Tek it out, nuh waan no strife.

Lef mi trunk bed,
Need fi lay mi tiad head,
Lef mi peacock spread,
Mi nuh need dat sheet instead.

Lef mi greeting cards,
An gallang a yuh yard,
Nuh touch dem schoolbook,
Children need dem fi look.

Nuh tek mi radio fusion,
Too much confusion,
No iPhone,
Mi wi send mi telegram.

Nuh tek mi ice box,
Mi nuh need dis freezer,
Nuh pull mi clothes line,
Mi nuh need no dryer.

Lef mi spike heel,
Mek mi feel so real,
Nuh tek mi abble frock,
Mi waan dress up inna dat.

Tek dis old handbag,
An gi mi wah yuh got,
Mi nuh care fi expense,
But mi love dem purse.

After all dem do fit,
Di color a mi frock,
Not dat mi a change,
But mi haffi look good inna church.

Author: Marjorie E. Edwards
Created: February 4, 2011

LIMITED VIEW

Tiday mek three years ago,
Mi tell yuh so!
Dat di plan was to
See a betta life in view!

Yuh answer to mi was no!
Yuh couldn't go wid di flow,
Yuh intention was not to mek
Di advance past yuh fus blow.

Guess in yuh limited view,
In mi, yuh si nuttin new,
Now yuh asking fi time to be,
Wat do yuh really want from mi?

Precious time is running out,
Wen I have to run to di next block,
Why should I ever tun back,
An wid yuh nonsense, adjust my clock?

Three years ago, yuh tell mi no,
Couldn't even si pass yuh own toes,
Dat's wen yuh choose to rebuff,
An now, yuh a come play tough?

Three years ago,
Yuh were not dat mature of a one,
Now yuh want fi make some plans,
Fi tek tings back into yuh hands.

Yuh a one good friend,
Beyond reasonable an all pretense,
But di limited view obstruct yuh sight,
Fi yuh fi si di upward flight.

Maybe it's time fi tek a real good try,
In everyting, mi honestly believe yuh wi comply,
But mi naw wait anadda three years again,
Just fi tell yuh goodbye!

Author: Marjorie E. Edwards
Created: December 22, 2010

FAREWELL
So Long

SORREL AT CHRISTMAS

For me, Christmas is a flavorful time,
High spirited, everyone getting into prime,
Even wid no money, everybody still a shine!
As part a di season, dere is some place fi dine.

Bustling, hustling, planting, an preparing,
All crops to be ready, di best time of sharing,
Tis di seasonal time wen every plant flourish,
Christmas is coming, enough time to accomplish.

Flowers deck every roadway,
Di aroma wi smell along di way,
Butterflies an birds sucking di pollen,
A smelling Christmas, everyone teking it all in.

All plants wid dem exploring beauties,
Just attracting di Christmas duties,
Everyting is in place to flourish,
It's dat time wen stress diminished.

Expectation to get everyting done an ready,
Fi Christmas to come an please everybody,
Families an friends joined up wen an wen,
Hoping fi si each odda, come next every year again.

Di drink from di sorrel,
Every year reaped in barrel,
Often times mi wonda fi a reason,
Would it flourish in any odda season?

But from mi sorrel garden tower,
Dis morning comes di fus flower,
 Planting at di right time is a blessing,
Wen it comes to sorrel pon time, it's no messing!

But di Christmas would be merrier,
If mi did plant it a while earlier,
Now it look like it nuh going be ready,
'Cause, di Christmas is dung pon wi already.

Christmas cake an sorrel drinks at Christmas
Di celebration in custom wi can always trust!
Wid God's love an blessing in abundance,
Di Christmas spirit brings joy an substance.

Any suggestions?

Author: Marjorie E. Edwards
Created: December 4, 2011

First bloom flower, sorrel and drink from my garden.

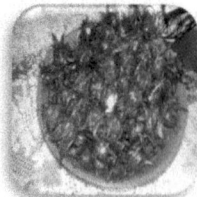

STRESS TO DEPRESS

Some tings in life really nuh call fah.
Talking bout too much to harbor,
Tings dat wi tek time fi interest,
Tun back pon wi wid stress to depress.

Tek fi instance too many bills,
Wish to cut dem out only if wi will,
Wi tek up too much pon wi head,
An it look like it a go kill wi dead!

Wi all a trying folks, yuh know,
Wi naa back dung, wi stand wi blow!
Trying fi fight it, get up an go,
Wid life's challenges, di vigor yuh mus show!

It a get tough an tougher dese days,
No matter how much yuh restructure yuh ways,
But here comes di time, fi join survival line,
An yuh haffi jump out deh truu rain or shine.

Wid so many tings fi do,
Money stiff an coming in few,
Hard fi succeed, not much afloat,
Whatever lickle come an yuh jump pon di boat.

An hope dat money will come about,
Wid enough fi pay di bills an di notes,
'Cause di minute yuh miss out pon dat route,
Yuh start getting some dreaded shouting out!

Some tings in life really nuh call fah,
Talking bout too much to harbor,
Tings dat wi tek time fi interest,
Tun back pon wi wid stress to depress*!*

Author: Marjorie E. Edwards
Created: October 6, 2011

DI BLOOD

Dem say Christian not to fight,
Dem not suppose fi get pon dat flight,
But dat nuh true,
After mi tell unno dis, unno going get di clue.

Dere was a Christian boy,
Who profess no lies,
Wen evil pon him flies,
In Jesus name, every ting 'im wi try.

One day oddas planned fi hurt 'im,
Not many friends fi 'im at school,
Dem planned to gang an beat 'im,
But fi 'im Jesus was ready an real.

Yuh nuh mess wid God's people,
Dem in di world but not of di world,
Dem consider blessed an peculiar,
But dese fools to dem was not familiar.

From a human point, di fear was dere,
But within 'im heart 'im was bold an dare,
No weapon but 'im faith an a red handkerchief,
An a God who stands in di midst's prepared.

Di boldest one come up bout fi touch,
Den 'im reach fi di red kerchief an flash!
As 'im flash 'im shout, Di blood! Di blood!
Lick dem wid Di blood! Di blood! Di blood!

Weh di power comes from, nobody knows,
'Im lash out hard wid some heavy blows,
'Im neva haffi use any gun,
Wid di red kerchief, di war was done.

It confused di whole band of fools,
Lickle Christian bwoy wid power double fold,
Dem fell over each odda from one to anadda,
Jesus blood lick dem straight pon di grung.

Dem sweats, groans, an even pass out cold,
Dem wonder wat di hell lick dem soul,
Fus one came alive, look lef den right 'Wh'appen?'
Di second one answered: "Wi surely got a whipping!"

God's pickney, unno nuh play with,
Dem lucky dat day di devil was invaded,
An as consciousness gain dem one by one,
Dem pick up foot, glad fi be alive, an scatter on.

Lickle Christian bwoy, a silent prayer to God,
Lawd, it's a shame fi dem it tun out so bad,
But fi mi Jesus' blood naw let mi dung,
An wid mi red kerchief, di victory won!

Author: Marjorie E. Edwards
Created: November 9, 2011

DI BRIDAL GOWN

Mi friend moved somewey out a town,
She's not tinking a coming back dung,
She had a job replacement,
So she had to reiterate!

She had someting up har sleeve,
Dat's why she neva say wen she lef,
Seems like she been at dat place before,
Den she went back to seek bout someting more!

Seemed like someone had grabbed har attention,
But wen we talked, she made no mention,
Mi wonda if she's living a secret life
Or she's trying to become somebody's wife!

One night she called mi out a choice,
Wid a crispy, clear, an happy voice,
Said she was standing on di outside,
Wid dis guy, to har, trying to serenade!

I neva know wat di plan was,
But she told mi a little later on, of course,
Dat 'im was har long time admirer,
An dat wid 'im she wants to be forever!

So to 'im, she let it be known,
 An dat man neva put up a frown,
'Im say, "Ok, if you want di bridal gown,
Den, I will not let you down!"

She did not want fi say anyting before,
Wanted to mek sure dat 'im love fi har was pure,
In addition dat har trip would not be in vain,
In di end, she end up wid a whole man to gain!

So har advice is wen yuh move inna a new town,
An yuh meet someone who enjoys being around,
Mek sure pon 'im face, 'im wears no heavy frown,
Wen 'im gives 'im heart in diamonds an di bridal gown!

Author: Marjorie E. Edwards
Created: March /2009

DIS DARN MOSQUITTA

Most time mi cyaan tek di baddaration,
Just wann fi sidung without any interruption,
Dis bold face mosquitta pon mi tek set,
An decide fi juice out all a wah mi get.

Mi see it a fly feverishly around,
Never know mi was its target bound,
Den mi feel it softly pitch dung,
As if mi was it's perfect sitting throne.

Seems like dis mosquitta always a figet,
Every time mi mek afta it, always a comeback,
Di itching, burning, an swollen mountain,
Pon mi hand, mi foot, even inna mi neck back.

One a di time, it fly up wid a rosy color,
Looking so richer dan di bill of a dolla,
Mi tink bout dat wicked disease, malaria,
Dis darn mosquitta a show mi say it superior!

Oh yea, yuh naa give up?
Today fi yuh is a very bad luck!
Enough, an yuh still waan more?
Coming back fi build mi a mountain a sores.

Den, wen mi look an si sinting red an black,
Mi sure no paat, a mi nuh look like dat,
An wid a big whop! "Eh eh!"
"Sorry, but mi cyaan allow yuh, fi suck weh mi fat!"

Author: Marjorie E. Edwards
Created: August 29, 2011

DI TASTE - DI CULTURE

Dem call it sexy, spicy, or exotic,
An wat do wi call it?
Hard work, di right proportion,
Dedication an supplication,
Wen it come to food fi people eat,
It mus taste good, fa a so wi dweet!

Wi done blessed as a nation,
So fortified in dat region,
Di food wi eat,
Di people wi greet,
Especial wen wi belly full,
Di best an biggest smile wi pull!

Di taste, Di culture wi cyaan figet it,
To di end a di world haffi talk bout it,
Just a taste an everyone waa fi eat it,
Wat a great treat!
Our food opens up di doors,
Wid wi love pure an sure!

Anywey yuh go run a boat,
Appetites crave an desires float,
Di aroma rides over seashores,
Get under crevices an gone truu doors,
Up inna di air, all put yuh in gear,
Watch yah, fi wi food lash out real an clear!

126

Cooking a pot,
Is no copycat,
Wi know wi spices,
Di real authentic choice,
Wid grace, di flavor fits in place,
Have wat it takes, none to replace!

Pon all di resources wi stand,
Sunshine an water, di land an man,
To complete di communion plan,
Food to put us in di right mood,
Di fruits come in any season it blooms,
Dem wonda how wi look so healthy in any form groomed!

Let's focus our mind an stick to di grace,
Wid fi wi taste, wi nuh haffi compete no race,
Wi know di right proportion fi blend in place,
Attracting thousands by thousands from any race,
To sit, dine, an in Jesus' name give di praise,
Wid fi wi food, kill it dead, already won di race!

Author: Marjorie E. Edwards
Created: November 8, 2011

YUH SI DI GAL DEH

Yuh si di gal deh, all looking shine,
Waiting fi wa, I don't know yuh mind.
Den someone else come an tief har heart,
Now yuh here, all falling apart.

Shud a speak up all yuh mind,
Before 'im tief har heart from behind.
Ih too late now dat she is gone,
Might as well yuh give up holding on.

Before yuh pop a kiss, an tell har di rest,
Yuh diddeh a wait till she gone attest,
Now mi nuh know wah fi tell yuh again,
'Cause yuh tears right now is all in vain.

Mi cyaan help yuh mi dear fren,
Yuh haffi go look anadda gal again.
Yuh be a man an stand up dis time,
An let no one else join in di line.

Use yuh heart right from di start,
An yuh wi know how fi play yuh part,
Tell har how much yuh love is boiling,
Even if she laughs, har heart will decide.

Betta fi wuk out yuh entire plan,
Dan end up losing to anadda man.
Dis time, mi friend, yuh wi cut di chase,
An save yuhself anadda heart of waste

Author: Marjorie E. Edwards
Created: September 6, 2011
128

Bereavement

A TRIBUTE TO MY SISTER

It all began, when two hearts came together as one,
The first baby girl came and grandma readily took charge,
She was like, "Go get your own, this one is mine!"
Two long-lonely years, waiting to see who would follow "Marge"

And lo, on a blessed August morn,
The second baby girl,
Most beautiful, bright-eyed little angel was born.
So it came to be, our mom, dad, grandma, my sister, and me.

A sister for us, and a cousin for more than just two,
We had a little fuss, but we all loved you,
From elder brother, the first that blessed the womb,
To youngest brothers, who later came in full bloom!

The yesteryears of our childhood dreams,
Were happily spent running down the river streams,
Catching janga shrimps, and watching dainty butterflies roam,
Protecting each other at school, on the busy streets, and at home.

Combing out the coconut hair of our glass bottle dolls,
With our own hair we twisted small "Chinese's Bump Balls,"
We cooked together, dishes galore, and in all varieties,
While grandma watched and supervised with solemn authority.

We played in the mud, and soaked in the fallen rain,
Then grandma dealt with the flu and aching pain,
We cracked sugar cane, and boy did we had fun!
Then got jealous, as the bird peck, into the apples under the sun.

The coconut limb was our main swing ride,
That lifted us from one end to the other side,
Didn't have to worry about our stupid weight,
We were just two little girls, relying on our fate.

Then there was the coconut bunka as our only skating board,
So far, those were the only toys that we could afford,
We sailed down the cleared hills with fearing chills,
Then scampered up again with our bunkas to get our refills.

Your principle was to show us the truth,
Out of your love came forth five progeny fruits,
For us to love, cherish, share, and pledge,
To continue the bonding unity that you had led.

So, sister dear, together, so many things we had shared,
Now that you choose no more to wait,
I'm certainly sure that those butterflies,
Are all waiting for you at Heaven's gate.

To escort you away to meet with your eternal date,
We knew that you were the strongest of us all,
But never thought that it would be this soon,
You would be invited to the Heavenly ball.

Not a loss, nor a defeat in battle,
It's like a birth in reverse,
For the same ones who welcomed you at birth, then,
Are all waiting there to welcome you home again.

You see, God works well with humble hearts,
When He looked around His garden path and saw the space,
Then He peeked down and saw your tired face,
So He reached out and saved you through His forgiving grace.

A sister we are all going to miss,
But a sister, we will have to release,
We are going to tie ourselves to you with our tears,
But grateful that together, we've had so many wonderful years.

I missed hearing your voice when we talked on the phone,
Especially when you answered, yes mi sister, in the humblest tone,
Your hugs, kisses, and beautiful welcoming smile are all gone.
Desolate, absent, empty, and without, the day when I came home.

With the pain we grieve for you, as we must,
We will be comforted by God's heavenly trust,
For only in a little while that we must part.
And the memories will be treasured in the depths of our hearts.

Author: Marjorie E. Edwards
Created: April 14, 2008 – April 18, 2008

Dedicated to my sister Authelyn Clarke (Peaches, Bev)
Gone but not forgotten
God rest her soul in peace

AS I KNEW HER

She was born a daughter and a sister,
Growing up, she glows and she glitters,
As young girls during our childhood days,
Our bonding was meant to make it in many ways.

She was very interesting, a unique and special left-hander,
While I, on the other side, am evenly ambidextrous,
To communicate we didn't have phone,
I doubt if we had ever heard a real dial tone.

We walked together most times to school,
And communicated with laid branches from the St. Vincent tool,
At times, one was ahead too fast,
But would surely meet up in our class.

We became humble wives, and mothers with babies,
Nurturing the substance and beauty of a lady,
In Christ, with enthused and committed fellowship,
We molded our children's hearts and minds in sacred purity.

Our friendships were sealed with special memories,
As mothers, sisters, and friends enjoying our families,
Life's journey drifted us distances apart,
But we held each other dearly within our hearts.

In the absence of my motherly ability,
As a couple, they became a tower of parental stability,
They didn't ask for money,
Wouldn't have made any difference if I had any.

Tia wrapped her arms around her five children so adoringly,
While Cleve went to work to provide, and maintain his family,
What a love, what a gift, what a true blessing in reality,
An avenue God worked for us to continue this bonding unity.

134

Thirteen Years Later

Together we cooked for our children,
Spent time with them as much as we could,
We talked about us as children growing up,
We talked about our babies holding up.

Individually, each one the special memories,
These things she had remembered out flat,
We had some great times, so grateful and thank God for that,
We are glad to have had her as a wife, a mommy and a friend.

She adored her children, and her children cherished her,
Whenever time she called for those who were not at home,
And failing to connect, she would call my phone,
In that tender voice she would ask, "Are my children OK?"

I've been trying to get them and it's all been a delay,
Yes sister dear, they're OK. I just spoke with them today,
A mommy, sister, and devoted friend, did her best to the end,
She taught me humility, as that special mom she'd been.

I'm glad to have given my first born as her daughter-in-law,
And in return she gave me her first born as my son-in-law,
So you see, this is not fiction but a true story,
Sisterly love without the biological blood, a story in its own glory.

Her Message

Before I go, I must tell you,
Before I go, I have to share with you,
Will you give me the attention,
For me to make my submission?
And tell you that I love you!

Will you take the time to share,
With others for whom I had cared?
In the many ways I had showed,
And tell them that I love them.
So before I go, I want you to know.

My family, friends, and all loved ones,
The time is here, the pain is gone,
New days are here as our God had declared,
I had fought the battle well,
Almost thirty years it had dwelled.

I am tired, so weak, exhausted I felt,
Can't keep up and I have to go,
I won't tell you not to try,
Because I know you going to cry,
But by then, I'll be way up high!

So dry your tears, try not to cry,
I know you want to keep me here,
But in God's own time, we'll meet over there,
My children, mom's love will always be here,
I leave with you God's comforting spirit from fear.

A love from a mother's heart intent,
Mommy who rocked you, sweet lullabies often spent,
Within these portals the memories will never end,
Do not question, or keep your thoughts suppressed,
God's wonders are the solutions of all trials complex.

Conclusion

As we celebrate the life of our sister,
Dearest sweet child of God,
Her joy comes after the raging tide,
Where among the heavens, holy angels abide,
God's precious love had called her to the other side,

Here we are left with the pain and grief we must,
But we will be comforted by God's heavenly trust,
When only for awhile that we all must part,
These precious memories will be cherished,
Deep within the depths of our very own hearts!

Author: Marjorie E. Edwards
Created: June 10, 2011

Dedicated to our dear sister, mother, wife and friend 'Sister Althea Smith' (Tia)
God rest her soul in peace

Author's Biography

Marjorie Elaine Edwards, affectionately called "Tuts," was born in the quiet district of Esher, in the Parish of Saint Mary, Jamaica W.I. as Marjorie Elaine Clarke. She attended the Esher Basic School, the Martin Top Elementary, and Martin All Age Schools.

Her attraction to poetry started at an early age, with four of the most outstanding people in her early childhood. First, her grandmother, Miss Alice Spencer, (God rest her soul), who sent Marjorie to school every morning, although was unable to read or write herself. Second, her basic schoolteacher, known to her as Miss Mack, with much patience taught her the letters of the alphabet, the importance of spelling, and writing well. Last, her All Age School teachers: Mrs. Mistelle Haughton and Mr. Alvin Parker helped to develop her imaginative observation in the areas of creative writing and acting. One of her favorite songs in school was "All Things Bright and Beautiful."

Marjorie was an active member of the Martin All Age School drama group. She represented her school at the competitive level in the Jamaica Cultural Development Commission Drama competitions in stage acting, dancing, and recital performances, and received several medals and certificates of merits. She attended the Jamaica National School of Drama during the late 1970s, where she studied drama, dancing, music, voice and speech, and acting. During this time, she excelled in the areas of creative writing and dramatic presentations.

Marjorie's passion for writing is perceived deep within her soul, as an expression of collective ideas that are designed to refresh the mind in any given situation. Her spiritual zeal has played a significant role in her intellectual conception.

Marjorie is a passionate writer and a perceptive reader in terms of creative and practical principles. She is a Realtor by profession who practices in the South Florida region, as well as a poet, and a recording artist.

Her words of expressions, as she had described them, *is like an eccentric dialogue between her passion and expression with conviction to inspire, motivate and soothe as a therapeutic formula.*

"Words From A Poet's Soul" with Marjorie E. Edwards, has featured on the Rich Davis Show, on WLVJ1040AM, and WBZT1230AM during 2010-2012, which made it into a household name. Rich Davis has been a consistent guidance and support with the compilation of combining her poems into the publication of this book.

Marjorie is the mother of three children: Tasha Lee, Gerald, and Larenio.
She has a son-in-law, Dwight, and a grandson, Deaundre. She currently resides in South Florida.

Jamaican Patois

Patois (Patwa) is a native style of expression predominantly used among Jamaicans to communicate on a social level. It is an English-lexified creole language with West African influences. It is the dominant language in Jamaica and the Diaspora community.

Here, are some examples with their meanings as used in the **Cultural Section.**

Abble frock	Close fitting knee length dress
Afta, An	After, And
Anadda	Another
Baddaration	Botheration
Bunka	Coconut or palm limb used to make skating board
Bwoy, Bway	Young man or teenager
Cyaan	Can't, Cannot
Cyan	Can
Dan	Than
Dat	That
De, Di	The
Di big life	The wealthy lifestyle
Deh -deh	There
Diddeh	There
Dem	Them
Dere	There
Dese	These
Dis	This
Dolla	Dollar
Dung	Down
Dweet	Do it
Eh Eh, Ere	Yes, Here
Escovitch	Spicy way of preparing fried fish
Fa,Fah	For
Fe wi, Fi wi	For us, Ours
Fi	For, To (wha fi tell yuh again)

Jamaican Patios Cont

Fi mi	For my, For I
Figet	Forget
Fren, Fret	Friend, Worry
Fus	First
Gal	Girl
Gallang	Go along
Gi mi	Give me
Go run a boat	Cooking Jamaican menu
Grung	Ground
Gwwwaaayyy	Go away
Haffi	Have to
Har	Her
Ih	It
'Im, Inna	Him, Into, In, Inside
Janga, Jus	River shrimps, Just
Lawd	Lord
Lef	Left
Likkle, Lickle	Little
Lick	Knock, Hit
Maskitta	Mosquito
Mek	Make
Mi, Me	Me, My, Mine
Mus	Must
Mm, Mm	Yes, Agreed
Nah, Naa	Not
Nedda, Neva,	Another, Never
Nuh	No, Not, Don't
Nuttin	Nothing
Odda	Other
Paat	Part
Papa	Father or older man
Pon	On
Pickney	Child, Children
Si, Sen, Sey	See, Sent, Say

Jamaican Patios Cont.

Shi	She
Sinting	Something
Sidung	Sit down
Still a shine	Living on, Survival
Tek	Take
Teet	Teeth, Tooth
Truu, Thru	Through
Tiad	Tired
Tief	Thief
Ting, Tink	Thing, Think
Togedda	Together
To	Too
Twangy way	To speak with a twang
Uno, unno	Everyone, All of you
Wen	When
Waan	Want
Wah, Wat	What
Wh'appen	What's happening
Weh	Away, Where
Wi	Will, (Mi wi send mi telegram)
Wi, We	Us, Ours
Wid	With
Wonda	Wonder
Wudda	Would
Wuk	Work
Wuss	Worst
Yah	Here
Yeye	Eye, Eyes
Yuh	You, Your

Acknowledgements

From the Author; The peace of God, which passeth all understanding shall keep our hearts and minds through Him.
Philippians 4:7 KJV

Special thanks to Rich Davis and the Rich Davis Show, whose brilliant idea became the title "Words From a Poet's Soul." Rich has been the vibrant and consistent source of constructive encouragements for me with the compilation of my poems to publish this book. I would also like to thank him for his support with exposure, motivation, appreciation, and the will to bring this cause to the world.

To Mr. and Mrs. Eugene Grey, who have added melody to my written words to bring "Words From a Poet's Soul to the next classical level.

To all the expertise from the different medias, who had worked behind the scenes in unity with professionalism to help with this production. For all your patience and winning efforts, I say thanks.

Thanks to my family and friends who have always been there for me with their support, prayers, laughter, and encouragements, patience and a whole lot more.

"Words from a Poet's Soul" have become such a sensational blessing for us, and we are extremely happy to share with gratitude to everyone who will read through the pages of this book.

Marjorie E. Edwards

References

Edwards, Marjorie E. (February, 2012). Words from a Poet's Soul. As a Jamaican by birth, my knowledge of the patios language is very well cultured. This book was written based upon the interpretation of my collective knowledge and my experiences both home and abroad as a member the Diaspora community. However, I did facilitated outside references to maintain a consistent dialogue.

Zuke, Ras. (2014). Rastafarian Vibrations. Retrieved from
    http://www.speakjamaican.com

Cooper, Kenneth J. (2009). Part of Speech. Retrieved from
    http://connection.ebscohost.com/c/articles/44641817/parts-
    speech
    Bryan, Beverley. (July 2004). Ethnic & Racial Studies.
    Retrieved from
    HTTP://ACADEMIC.RESEARCH.MICROSOFT.COM/AUTHOR/35318977/
    BEVERLEY-BRYAN

Pictures were photographed by Marjorie E. Edwards using Galaxy S3 Android phone camera with an 8.0 mega pixel resolution.

Images were designed, and created with MacOS X iPhoto, Micro Soft Word Doc., Picture Management, Video Maker, Window Live Photo Gallery, Window Photo Viewer, and Word Art Software Applications.

Kingston Harbor. Jamaica W. I.

Please visit us at www.marjorieeedwards.com for more
inspirational products.

Thanks for your generous contributions.

THE END

www.ingramcontent.com/pod-product-compliance
Lightning Source LLC
Chambersburg PA
CBHW070808100426
42742CB00012B/2299